THE

Bones
GameBook
& SKELETON

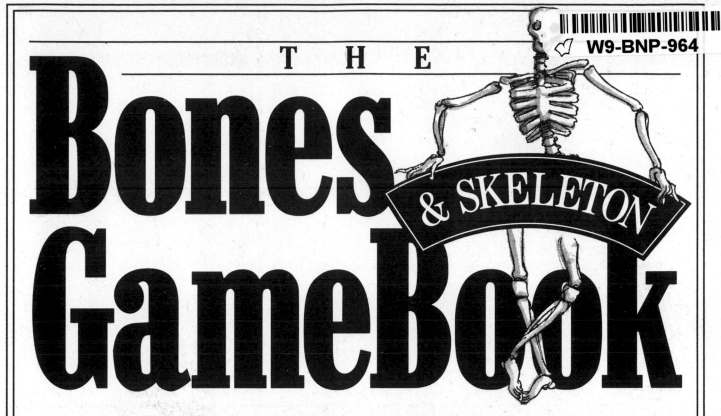

By Karen C. Anderson and Stephen Cumbaa

Somerville House Publishing
Toronto

Published by Somerville House Publishing
a division of Somerville House Books Limited
3080 Yonge Street, Suite 5000
Toronto, Ontario M4N 3N1

Published simultaneously in the United States by Workman Publishing,
New York

Canadian Cataloguing in Publication Data

Cumbaa, Stephen L.
    The bones and skeleton gamebook

ISBN: 0-921051-54-9 (unit)
ISBN: 0-921051-68-9 (counterpack)

1. Scientific recreations—Juvenile literature. 2. Bones—Juvenile litera-
ture. 3. Human skeleton—Juvenile literature. 4. Body, Human—
Juvenile literature. 5. Human anatomy—Juvenile literature.
I. Anderson, Karen C. II. Title
QM 101.C85 1993
j612.7'5
C93-094545-X

Special thanks to the Canadian Museum of Nature, Ottawa, Canada

Canadian
Museum
of Nature

Musée
canadien
de la nature

Printed in the United States of America

Somerville House Publishing acknowledges the financial assistance
of the Ontario Publishing Centre, the Ontario Arts Council,
the Ontario Development Corporation and the Department of
Communications.

DEDICATION

To my parents, for their inspiration and love—and the foresight to have chosen medical careers so that they could help me in the preparation of this book.

Karen C. Anderson

To my parents, Bill and Carolyn, for fostering my curiosity with continuing love and encouragement, and to my grandmother Mimi, who inspires me with her tenacity, grace and good humor.

Stephen Cumbaa

Contents

Introduction 5
Boning Up 7

CHAPTER 1: THE BONE ZONE
    Bones to Pick 10
    Meet Me at the Joint 11
    Twist and Shout! 12
    Rubber Bones 14
    A Pile of Bones 15
    Inside Out 16

CHAPTER 2: MUSCLE BOUND
    Muscle Mambo 18
    Brainless Moves 19
    Chair Lift 20
    Handy Dandy 21
    Hands Up! 22

CHAPTER 3: BODY PARTS
    Organ-ization 24
    Organ Grinders 25
    Playing with Instruments 26
        Thumping Noises 27
    Name Calling 28
    Physical Examination 30

Body Language 32
Have Patients 33
How Much, How Many? 34

CHAPTER 4: COVER-UPS
    Prints Charming 36
        Powder Prints 37
        Get a Grip 37
    Sweaty Palms 38
    Hairy Tales 39
        Hairs to You! 39
    Pressure Points 40
        Tickle, Tickle 40

CHAPTER 5: THE SENSE OF IT ALL
    Hear, Hear! 42
        Tuning Up 43
        Spinning Around 43

In One Ear and In the Other 44
Come to Your Senses 45
Light Show 46
   Star Light, Star Bright 47
Now You See It, Now You Don't!....48
   What Big Eyes You Have! 48
3-D 49
Hole-in-One 50
   See Here! 50
The Nose Knows—or Does It?......51
What's That Smell? 52
Taste Tests 54
   Fuzzy Tongue! 55
Jog Your Memory 56
Total Recall 58

CHAPTER 6: ALL SYSTEMS GO
Watering Holes 60
Just Picture It! 62
Secret Ingredients........................64

The Whole Tooth 65
Sound Bites..................................66
The Hard Facts............................67
Apple Adventure 68
Gulp!..69
Three-Letter Words 70
Matters of the Heart 71
Go With the Flow 72
Wise Guys....................................73
Artificial Respiration....................74
   All Steamed Up 75
All Together Now! 76

CHAPTER 7: BODY WORKS
Blue Genes....................................78
   Genetic Code 79
Bodily Myths 80
Little Man 81
Is There a Doctor in the House?...82
Dizzying Heights............................84
   Morning Stretch 85
Balance of Power..........................86

ANSWERS 87

FEEL IT IN YOUR BONES

The more you learn about your body, the more you can appreciate its miraculous design. You already know that your bones give you shape, but did you know that muscles move your bones and that nerves move your muscles? Can you guess which part of your body regulates all this activity, and nearly everything else that goes on inside you?

It's all here: cells and organs, systems and senses, teaming up to keep you on the go. You'll learn what your stomach looks like, why you sweat, how long it takes your hair to grow and where your taste buds are. You'll find out how you keep your balance, why you can't see in the dark and who made off with the cookies in the cookie jar (page 37).

Page after page, you'll find word games and picture puzzles, mazes and match-ups, solo experiments and projects with partners—even tricks and illusions that will amaze your family and friends. And when you're done, you can turn to the answer section to find as much fun (no fair peeking).

So sharpen your pencil—and your wits—and come play with us in the Bone Zone!

BONING UP

The adult human skeleton comprises more than 200 bones! The most important ones are shown here, along with their common and scientific names. Sherlock Bones wants you to know that you'll need them for clues . . .

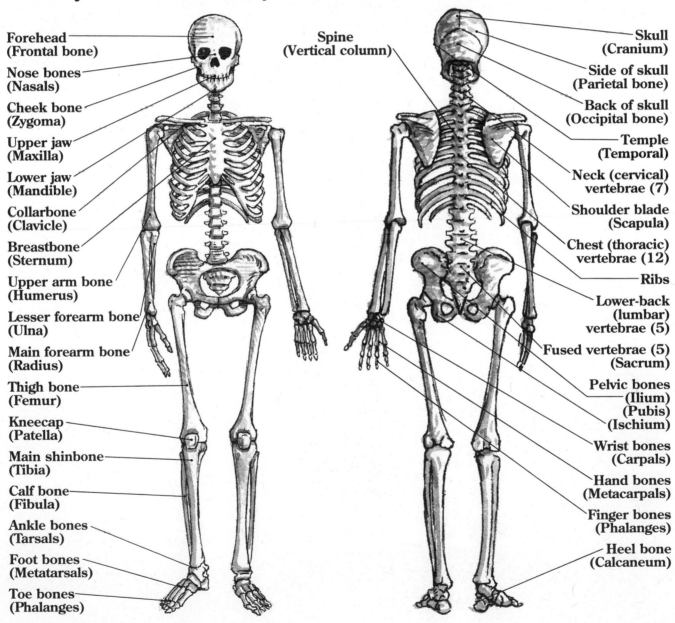

Forehead
(Frontal bone)

Nose bones
(Nasals)

Cheek bone
(Zygoma)

Upper jaw
(Maxilla)

Lower jaw
(Mandible)

Collarbone
(Clavicle)

Breastbone
(Sternum)

Upper arm bone
(Humerus)

Lesser forearm bone
(Ulna)

Main forearm bone
(Radius)

Thigh bone
(Femur)

Kneecap
(Patella)

Main shinbone
(Tibia)

Calf bone
(Fibula)

Ankle bones
(Tarsals)

Foot bones
(Metatarsals)

Toe bones
(Phalanges)

Spine
(Vertical column)

Skull
(Cranium)

Side of skull
(Parietal bone)

Back of skull
(Occipital bone)

Temple
(Temporal)

Neck (cervical)
vertebrae (7)

Shoulder blade
(Scapula)

Chest (thoracic)
vertebrae (12)

Ribs

Lower-back
(lumbar)
vertebrae (5)

Fused vertebrae (5)
(Sacrum)

Pelvic bones
(Ilium)
(Pubis)
(Ischium)

Wrist bones
(Carpals)

Hand bones
(Metacarpals)

Finger bones
(Phalanges)

Heel bone
(Calcaneum)

Chapter 1

The Bone Zone

Bones to Pick
Meet Me at the Joint
Twist and Shout!
Rubber Bones
A Pile of Bones
Inside Out

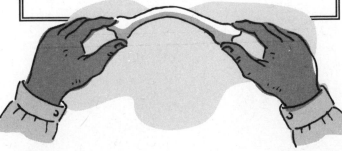

Bones to Pick

Five skeletons have just come off the assembly line at the Bone Yard skeleton factory. Unfortunately, only two will pass inspection; the other three are flawed. If you were in charge, which skeletons would you mark as "rejects"—and why?

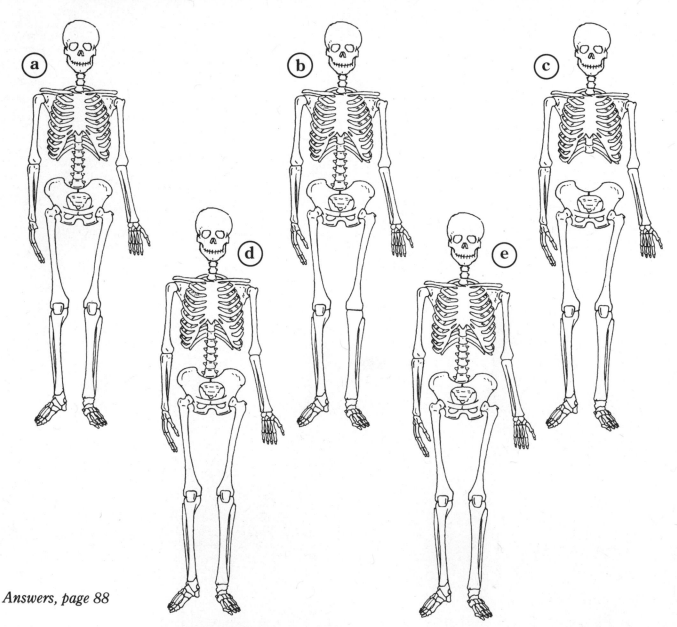

Answers, page 88

Meet Me at The Joint

The owner of The Joint, a fast-food establishment in the town of Bony Corners, wants to open seven new franchises with the following names:

1. **The Knuckle Joint**
2. **The Wrist Joint**
3. **The Ankle Joint**
4. **The Knee Joint**
5. **The Shoulder Joint**
6. **The Elbow Joint**
7. **The Hip Joint**

Since all the main streets in town are named for bones and laid out just like a human skeleton, with corners representing the joints where two bones meet, the town planners had no trouble deciding where each fast-food Joint should go. (For instance, The Hip Joint belongs where Femur meets Ischium.) Can you place the other new Joints?

PHALANGES
SCAPULA
METACARPALS
HUMERUS
RADIUS/ULNA
CARPALS
⑦
ISCHIUM
FEMUR
TIBIA/FIBULA
TARSALS

Twist and Shout!

After performing these two tricks, you won't have any doubts about how supple your arms are—thanks to the joints at your wrists and elbows. The first trick is designed to fool the brain; the second creates an illusion that will fascinate your friends.

1. Crossed Signals

Cross your arms in front of you, then put your palms together and fold your hands. Now, with your fingers locked, bend your elbows and pull your hands under and back up to the front of your chest. Ask someone to point to one of your fingers. Try to move that finger.

Not so easy, is it? See if the other person fares any better!

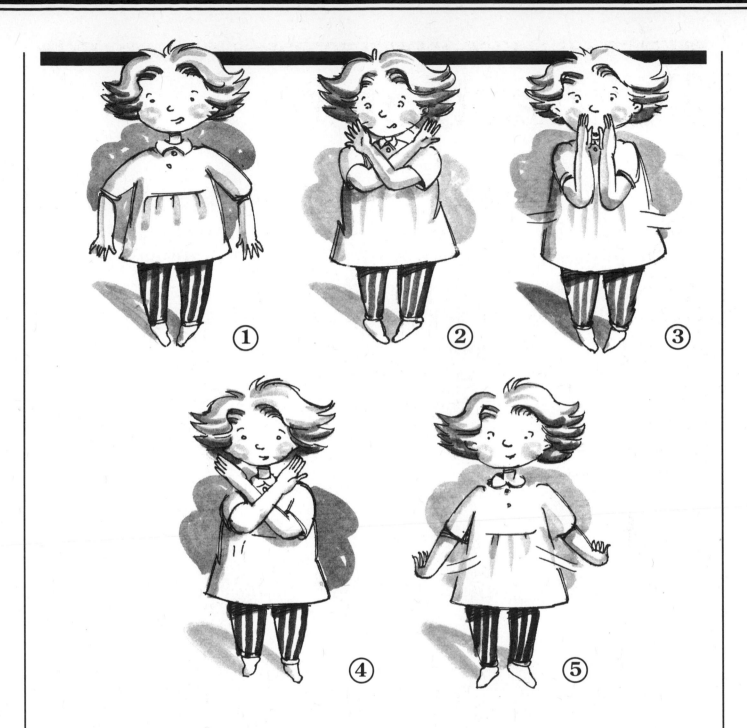

2. Spinning Elbows

Stand in front of a mirror with your hands out to the side (1). Swing your arms up to your chest so that they cross at the elbow (2). Now, keeping your elbows together, slide your wrists across each other (3) and follow through until your arms are crossed with the opposite arm on top (4). Let your arms flop down as you uncross them and swing them back out to the side (5). Repeat. It should look as if your arms are spinning at the elbows.

Practice the motions until they're smooth and quick, then call in your audience.

Rubber Bones

Two minerals, called calcium and phosphorus, are responsible for producing sturdy bones to replace the soft cartilage that formed your skeleton when you were born. By the time you're 20 years old, their job will be done—but you'll still have to keep up your mineral supply! To see for yourself what happens to bones if you deprive them of minerals, try the following experiment.

You will need:

- Chicken or turkey bones
- 2 jars or water glasses
- Water
- Vinegar

water   vinegar

Strip the bones clean and let them dry out overnight. Next, submerge one bone in a jar of water and the other in a jar of vinegar. Let the bones soak for 3 days, then remove them from the jars. Try to bend the bone that was in the water. Now try to bend the bone that was in the vinegar.

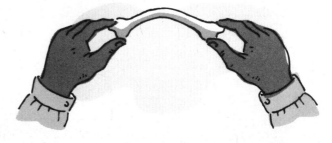

The vinegar-soaked bone has softened because its minerals have dissolved in acid. Can you tie it in a knot? If not, let it sit in vinegar for a few more days and try again.

A Pile of Bones

Each of the picture-names below contains the word BONE or BONES. How many pictures can you identify before you become BONE-tired?

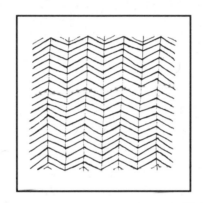

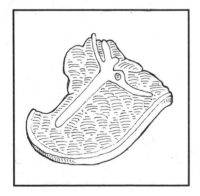

Answers, page 88

Inside Out

Three-fourths of all the animals in the world, including insects and crustaceans, grow skeletons outside their bodies. These stiff *exoskeletons* are good for jumping and swimming, but they prohibit all the amazing twists and turns that our own skeletons permit.

Connect the dots below to find an animal that wears its skeleton on the outside.

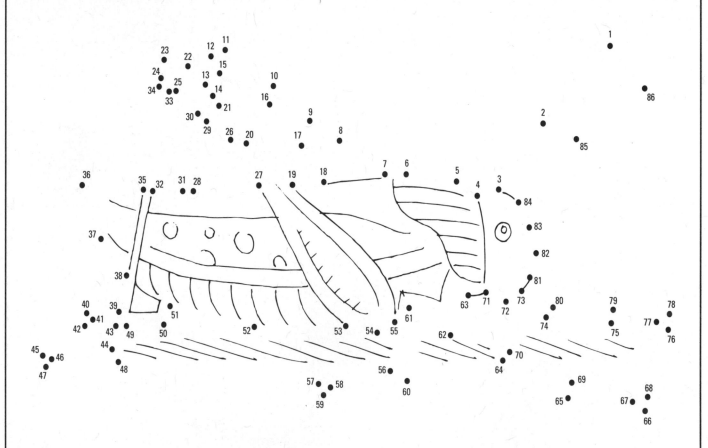

I am a _____ .

Chapter 2
Muscle Bound

Muscle Mambo
Brainless Moves
Chair Lift
Handy Dandy
Hands Up!

Muscle Mambo

Muscle fibers are always either contracted or relaxed—there's no "in between." And they can only contract for a fraction of a second at a time. So, even when you think you're as still as a statue, your muscles might be twitching like crazy!

You will need:

- A twist tie
- A ruler (or a stick)
- A table

Fold the twist tie in half and slip it over one end of the ruler. Now hold the ruler over the table. Without supporting your arm, try to keep the twist tie as close to the table and as steady as possible. In a few seconds, the tie will start to "dance" in time with your muscle contractions.

Of the 650 or so muscles that cover your skeleton, the longest is the sartorius muscle in your thigh. Can you guess where the smallest muscles are? (<u>Hint:</u> They're attached to the smallest bones in your body.)

Answers, page 89

Brainless Moves

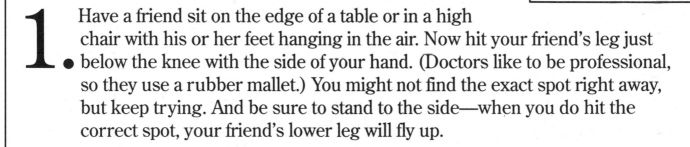

Reflexes are muscular reactions to messages that stop short of the brain. Reactions like blinking and ducking can save us from getting something harmful in our eyes or being hit on the head.

Doctors test your reflexes to make sure the spinal part of your nervous system, where these messages are handled, is working correctly. Here are some ways you can watch reflexes in action.

1. Have a friend sit on the edge of a table or in a high chair with his or her feet hanging in the air. Now hit your friend's leg just below the knee with the side of your hand. (Doctors like to be professional, so they use a rubber mallet.) You might not find the exact spot right away, but keep trying. And be sure to stand to the side—when you do hit the correct spot, your friend's lower leg will fly up.

2. If you have a dog, or a friend with a dog, it's fun to test the leg reflex. Get the dog to roll over on its back, then rub its belly toward the bottom of the rib cage and over to the side of the leg that's up in the air. If you get it right, the leg will start rotating as if the dog were actually running!

Chair Lift

It's true that boys are born with more muscle fiber than girls, but muscles aren't everything! Just watch what happens when you challenge male family members or friends to perform this chair exercise.

First try it out yourself, following these steps.

You will need:

- A straight-backed chair
- A partner

1. Face the wall, touching it with your toes, then take 2 paces backwards and put your feet together.

2. Ask your partner to place the chair between you and the wall.

3. Lean forward until your forehead touches the wall. Let your arms hang straight down, with your hands just above the sides of the chair.

4. Now, in one fell swoop, try to lift the chair as you stand up straight. If you're a girl, you won't have any trouble lifting the chair; if you're a boy, however, the chair probably won't budge. The answer lies in your body's *center of balance*, which is lower in girls and women than in boys and men.

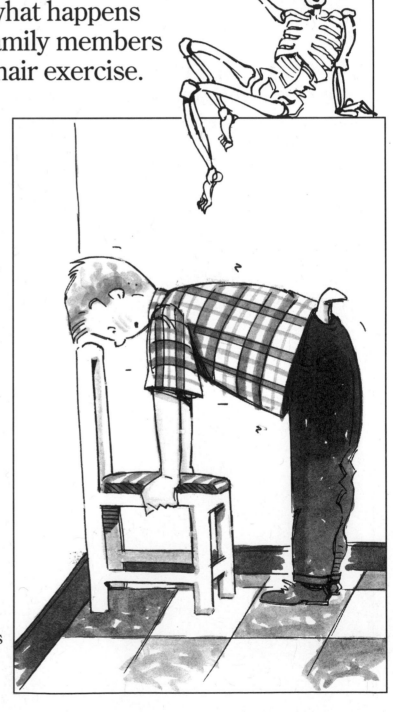

Handy Dandy

Before modern machines and conveniences, most of our work and play depended on our hands. (Did you know that "handy" first meant "easy to fit in your hand"? Or that "handsome" used to mean "good with your hands"?) Examine the scene below, then try your own hand at finding all the objects and activities whose names include the word HAND.

Answers, page 89

Hands Up!

Sometimes your body appears to have a mind of its own, when it's actually following orders. Stand in a doorway and press your arms against both sides of the opening. Push as hard as you can for a couple of minutes, until you feel yourself shaking from the strain. Now step out of the doorway and watch your arms rise.

Messages were still on their way from your brain to your arms, telling them to move up and out—even though you'd stopped pushing!

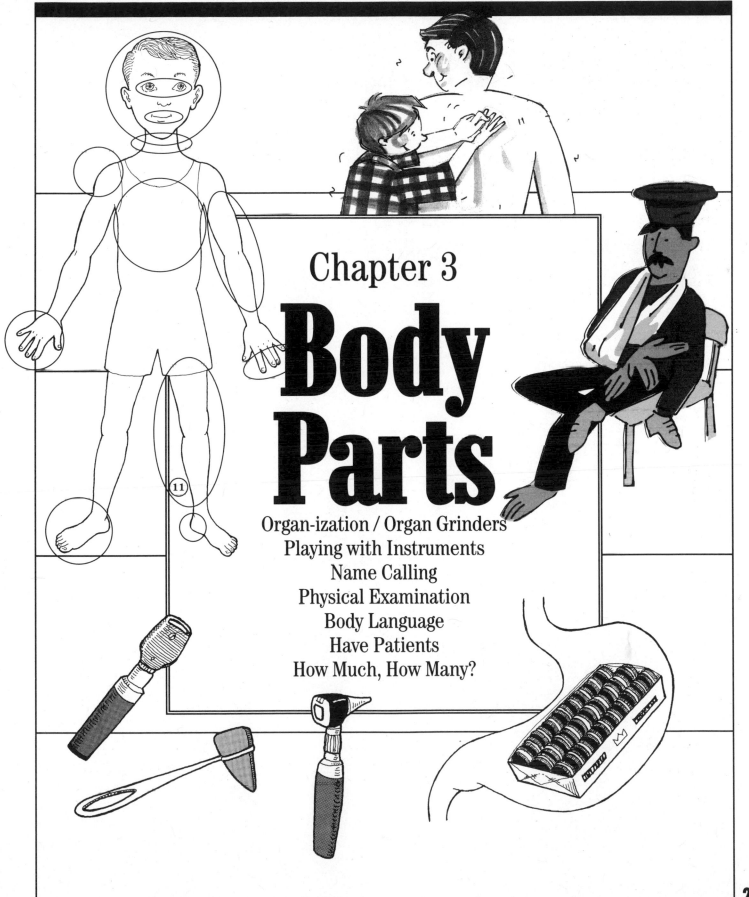

Chapter 3

Body Parts

Organ-ization / Organ Grinders
Playing with Instruments
Name Calling
Physical Examination
Body Language
Have Patients
How Much, How Many?

Organ-ization

Four organs of the human body appear in silhouette below. The names of the organs are scrambled at the bottom of the page. Can you unscramble each name and then match it to the correct shadow?

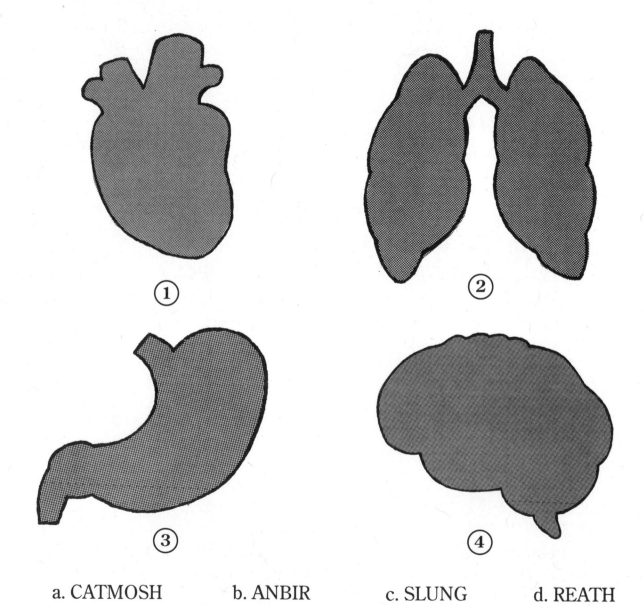

① ② ③ ④

a. CATMOSH   b. ANBIR   c. SLUNG   d. REATH

Answers, page 89

Organ Grinders

Here's a quick quiz on body organs. We don't expect you to know all the answers—just use your common sense and your sense of humor!

1. Your stomach can stretch to hold how much food?
  a. One pint
  b. One quart
  c. One gallon
  d. One package of Oreos

2. How big would you guess each of your lungs is?
  a. The size of a golf ball
  b. The size of a baseball
  c. The size of a football
  d. The size of a basketball

3. Which is your largest internal organ?
  a. Liver
  b. Lungs
  c. Stomach
  d. Skin

4. At rest, your heart beats approximately how many times per minute?
  a. Under 10 times
  b. 75 times
  c. 750 times
  d. Over 100,000 times

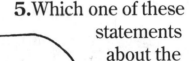

5. Which one of these statements about the brain is false?
  a. The right half of your brain controls the left side of your body and vice versa.
  b. The larger your brain, the more intelligent you are. (According to *The Guinness Book of World Records,* Einstein's brain is one of the biggest brains ever measured.)
  c. Operations on the brain can be performed with a local anaesthetic because the brain contains so few nerves.
  d. Even though computers can accomplish several million calculations per second, there is no computer that can beat a chess master in a game of chess.

Answers, page 89

Playing with Instruments

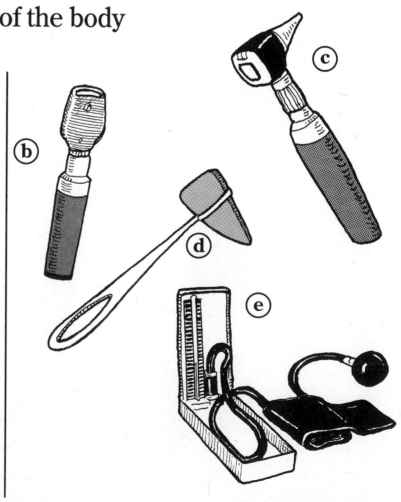

Five medical instruments are spread out on this page. Some you'll probably recognize right away, while others may look like ancient torture devices!

Using your knowledge and the process of elimination, try to match each instrument to its name at the left and also to the appropriate parts of the body on the facing page.

- **otoscope**
- **stethoscope**
- **ophthalmoscope**
- **sphygmomanometer**
- **reflex hammer**

①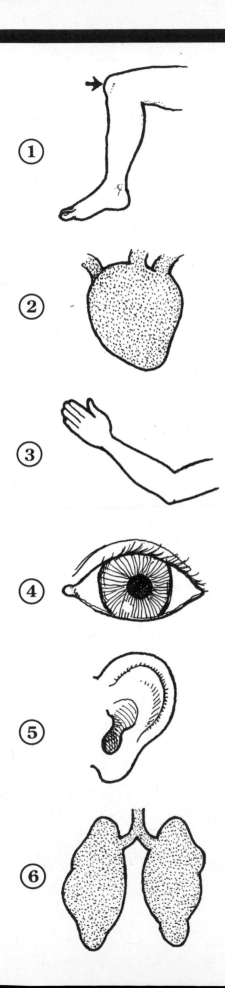

②

③

④

⑤

⑥

THUMPING NOISES

Do you remember the doctor tapping your back during an exam? This technique, called "percussing," gives a good picture of what's going on under your skin. (A muffled sound from your lungs, for example, instead of the normal hollow sound, might indicate unwanted fluid in the area.) It works a lot like finding a stud, or wooden support, in a wall; if you knock every few inches, you'll hear the sounds change from high and hollow to low and solid whenever you come to a stud.

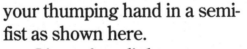

To percuss: Enlist a "patient" and place one hand flat on his or her body. Knock the middle finger of that hand sharply with the middle finger of your other hand; hold your thumping hand in a semi-fist as shown here.

Listen for a lighter, vibrating noise when you tap a bony place, such as the shoulder blades or ribs; a hollow thud for an air-filled cavity as in the lungs or an empty stomach; and a dull knock for muscle such as the biceps or thigh.

Good listening!

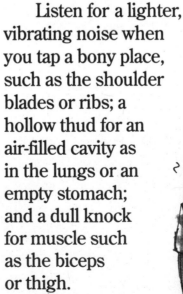

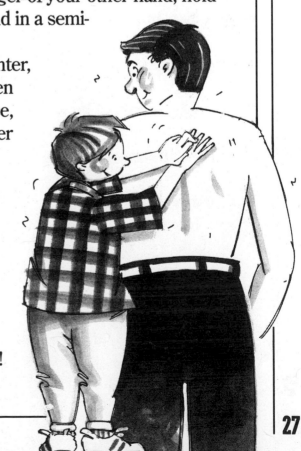

Name Calling

The names for parts of the body can tell some interesting stories. For instance, the word *biceps* means "two heads" (the biceps muscle has two places at the top where it connects to bone).

Here's a quiz on some of the more peculiar names associated with the body. Make your best guesses.

1. **The hippocampus** (sea horse)
   a. is located in the brain's limbic system and plays a role in learning and memory. It looks like a sea horse.
   b. is a tiny bone in the joint of the thumb. It looks like a sea horse.
   c. is part of the pancreas (which looks like a sea horse), specializing in secreting a hormone that speeds up metabolism.
   d. is a special university for large aquatic mammals.

2. **Osteoblast**
   a. means "bone breaker" and refers to the acids in foods like soda pop that extract calcium from bones.
   b. means "ear breaker" and is a bacterium that can infect the eardrum and cause deafness.
   c. means "bone maker" and describes the type of cell that helps repair damaged bone and create new bone tissue.
   d. means "Get out of the way, someone's exploding dynamite in the cemetery!"

3. **Pinna**
   a. means "little pin" and is used by surgeons to help piece together small bits of broken bone.
   b. means "feather" or "wing" and refers to the ear lobe.
   c. means "sheet" and is part of the large, wide muscle that extends across the face and helps us smile.
   d. was one of Columbus' ships that sailed across the Atlantic Ocean in 1492.

4. **The cauda equina** (horsetail)
   a. is the spindly bunch of nerve fiber ends that hang down from the spinal cord.
   b. is the technical name for the "funny bone" nerve near your elbow.
   c. is the name of the gland that stimulates growth of facial hair on men.
   d. is a fancy new name for a ponytail.

5. **Solar plexus**
   a. means "sun problem" and refers to a condition in the eye caused by too much bright light.
   b. means "star-shaped nerve fibers" and is located behind the stomach.
   c. means "sun network" and refers to the tiny tentacles of capillaries that spread out to cover the liver.
   d. is the urge to sneeze when sunbathing.

6. **The Islets of Langerhorn**
   a. are the places in the pancreas where insulin is secreted.
   b. are the spots in the brain where déjà vu takes place.
   c. are little openings in the cheeks and soft palate that allow saliva to seep into the mouth.
   d. is the site of a famous clinic where people go to lose weight.

7. **Malleus**
   a. means "evil one" and refers to any virus that invades the body.
   b. means "hammer," the shape of a tiny bone in the ear.
   c. means "clay-like" and describes the part of bone marrow that can be molded and shaped when extracted.
   d. is the nauseous feeling that results from overeating.

8. **Duodenum**
   a. means "connected twice" and describes the ankle joint.
   b. means "two times two" and refers to the part of the brain where groups of nerves cross over from one side to the other.
   c. means "twelve each" ("twelve-finger width") and is the first part of the small intestine (about 10 inches long).
   d. refers to the latest fad of wearing two pairs of jeans, one on top of the other.

Answers, page 90

Physical Examination

Each picture on the facing page has the same name as a part of the body. How many can you match to one of the circled body parts shown here? We've filled in one part to get you started.

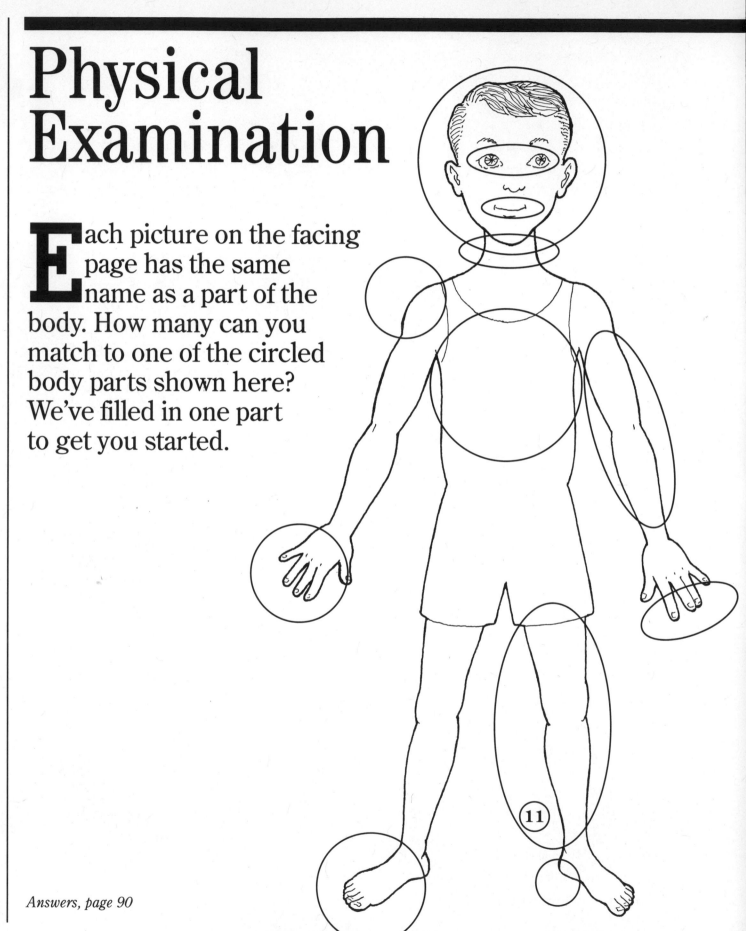

Answers, page 90

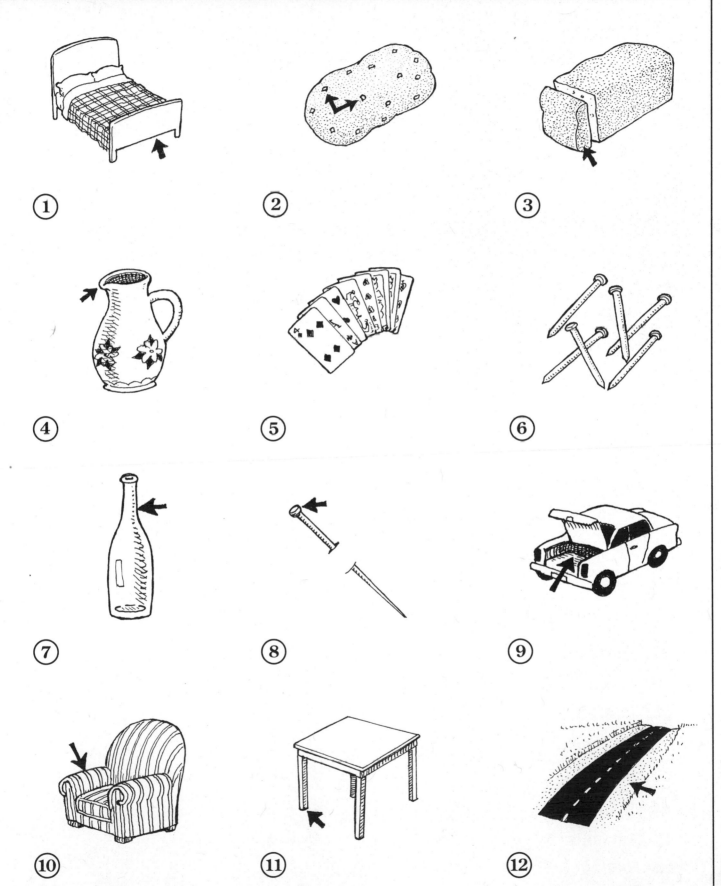

① ② ③

④ ⑤ ⑥

⑦ ⑧ ⑨

⑩ ⑪ ⑫

Body Language

When you overhear doctors talking to each other, do you sometimes think they're speaking a foreign language? In a sense, they are! The scientific names for many of our body parts are Greek or Latin—or at least rooted in these two languages. How many of the scientific names on the left below can you match to the common names on the right?

1. scapula	a. thumb
2. patella	b. voice box
3. pollex	c. windpipe
4. thorax	d. breastbone
5. larynx	e. collarbone
6. clavicle	f. kneecap
7. tympanum (tympanic membrane)	g. shinbone
8. nares	h. tailbone
9. tibia	i. shoulder blade
10. coccyx	j. chest
11. epidermis	k. finger bone
12. sternum	l. jawbone
13. trachea	m. skin
14. phalanx	n. nostrils
15. mandible	o. eardrum

Answers, page 90

Have Patients

No, nothing's wrong with your eyes! There are several things ailing this doctor's office and waiting room. (For example, the stool is standing on only three legs.) Can you detect at least 10 abnormalities and restore the scene to normal?

Answers, page 91

How Much, How Many?

Some of the amounts of things in and on your body are very surprising. For instance, even though you look naked in your birthday suit, your body is covered by a "coat" of more than four million hairs!

Can you match the amounts on the left with the items on the right?

1. 1.2 to 1.6 gallons	**a.** Amount of blood in the body
2. 1,000	**b.** Capacity of the bladder
3. 2,000 to 3,000 gallons	**c.** Length of the small intestine
4. 60%	**d.** Number of new red blood cells made per second
5. 2.5 pints	**e.** Amount of water sweated per day
6. 44 gallons	**f.** Number of nerve endings in one square inch of skin
7. 16%	**g.** Amount salivated per day
8. 15 to 30 feet	**h.** Amount of air an adult breathes per day
9. 1 to 1.5 pints	**i.** Percentage of body weight that is water
10. 14%	**j.** Percentage of body weight that is skin
11. 1 to 2 quarts	**k.** Percentage of body weight that is bone
12. 2 to 3 million	**l.** Amount of water that passes through the kidneys per day

Answers, page 91

Every hour, you shed about a million skin cells. In fact, most of the dust in your home (unless you have a lot of hairy pets) is composed of dead skin!

Chapter 4
Cover-Ups

Prints Charming
Sweaty Palms
Hairy Tales
Pressure Points

Prints Charming

Your fingerprints are unique. No one else in the world has the same patterns of ridges on the "bulbs" of their fingers. (Even identical twins have nonidentical prints!)

To see your fingerprints clearly, you'll need a stamp pad and blank paper. Press each finger, one at a time, first on the pad and then on the paper. Label each print.

Now compare your prints with the patterns below.

whorl

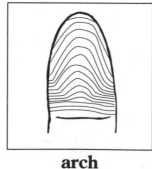
arch

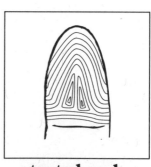
tented arch

double loop

ulnar loop

radial loop

Powder Prints

Using the stamp pad and paper, take the finger-prints of friends or family members. Next, ask one of them to lift and move an object like a cookie jar while you're out of the room. Will you be able to track down the culprit?

You will need:

- Baby powder
- See-through tape (the wider, the better)
- A piece of dark-colored paper

Dust the surface with powder. (Real investigators don't use baby powder, but it works fine.) Carefully blow off the excess powder, and you should see the outlines of at least one fingerprint.

Hold a strip of tape above the clearest print and lower it gently. Smooth out the tape to remove any air bubbles and be careful not to smear. Then lift up the strip and tape it down on the paper. Compare this fingerprint to the ones in your file, and you can prove who made off with the goods!

GET A GRIP!

The little ridges that make your fingerprints (and footprints) provide your skin with a non-skid surface.

Try this test: Place a piece of writing paper flat on a table and push it into a bump with the tips of your fingers. Don't put pressure on the table; just push lightly.

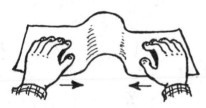

Now try to push the paper into a bump by using the backs of your hands. Again, don't apply any pressure; just move your hands toward each other.

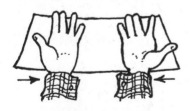

See how helpless we'd be if the "bulbs" of our fingers were as smooth as the backs of our hands?

Sweaty Palms

Maybe you think sweating is ugly and stinky. Well, it may be (especially on some people!), but sweat helps you to maintain the right temperature by carrying heat out of your body. To feel how it can cool you down, put on one wet sock and one dry sock on a very hot day.

You have sweat glands all over you, more in some places than others. To pinpoint a bunch of these glands in your hand, do the following experiment.

You will need:
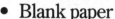

- Blank paper
- 2 teaspoons of cornstarch
- ½ cup of water
- Iodine

First cut the paper into small, palm-size squares. Mix the cornstarch with the water, and dunk the paper squares. Let the squares dry. Paint your palms with a thin layer of iodine.

Now do something that will make you sweat—go up and down the stairs quickly, jump rope or do some exercises that take a lot of energy. When you've worked up a good sweat, press one of the paper squares onto your palm. Peel it off and look for the dark spots on the paper. These spots mark the places where your sweat glands open up on the surface of your skin.

Hairy Tales

A little knowledge about the body and some basic math can shed new light on an old story. Use the facts at the right to answer the questions below.

In the story of Rapunzel, a fair maiden is trapped in a tower until a prince comes along and rescues her by climbing up a rope made of her hair.

If Rapunzel's hair hangs down 100 feet, what is her age at the time of her rescue? (Let's assume her hair never falls out, as most hair does after 2 to 6 years.) And how heavy can the prince be and still support himself by the 100,000 hairs on Rapunzel's head?

HAIRS TO YOU!

● Hair looks smooth and soft, especially in ads for shampoo, but it's actually made of a fibery protein called keratin and the surface of each hair is scaly.

Hair

Skin

Follicle

● Do you ever get so bored that you feel as if you're watching your hair grow? Can you guess how long it *really* takes to notice longer hair? In 2 months, hair grows about an inch.

● As you might know from cleaning out your brush, hair is a very strong material. A single strand of hair can support 2.8 ounces. A rope of 1,000 strands can hold up to 175 pounds (the weight of one large man).

Answers, page 91

Pressure Points

In the top layer of your skin are four different kinds of nerve endings, called sensors, that send information about touch, pressure, temperature and pain to your brain.

Try pinching a big chunk of skin on your upper arm. You'll probably only feel pressure. Now pinch a smaller fold of skin on your lower arm. This time, you'll probably feel pain. The sensors that detect pain are closer to the surface than those that respond to pressure.

Try this test: First enlist a friend. Then, while your friend's eyes are closed, open a paper clip and run the two end points down the length of his or her arm, all the way to the tip of the middle finger. Your friend will say it felt like only one point until it reached the hand. This is because the touch receptors are closer together on the hands and fingers than on the arms.

Let someone else tickle your ribs, and you're rolling on the floor in no time. But try to tickle yourself, and nothing happens—your nervous system knows what's coming and won't let you be taken by surprise.

Of all the parts of the body, which would you say has the most touch receptors?

Answer, page 91

Chapter 5

The Sense of It All

Hear, Hear!
In One Ear and In the Other
Come to Your Senses
Light Show
Now You See It, Now You Don't!
3-D
Hole-in-One
The Nose Knows—or Does It?
What's That Smell?
Taste Tests
Jog Your Memory

Hear, Hear!

Sound is made of vibrations, called sound waves, that enter the outer ear and travel through the middle ear to the inner ear before reaching the hearing centers in your brain. The volume (loudness) of a sound depends on the height of the waves; its pitch (high or low) depends on their frequency. Tone is the special quality of a sound. For instance, a violin and a horn can play a note with the same loudness and pitch, but each makes an entirely different sound.

Semicircular Canals

Hammer

Anvil

Eardrum

Auditory Nerve

Cochlea

Stirrup

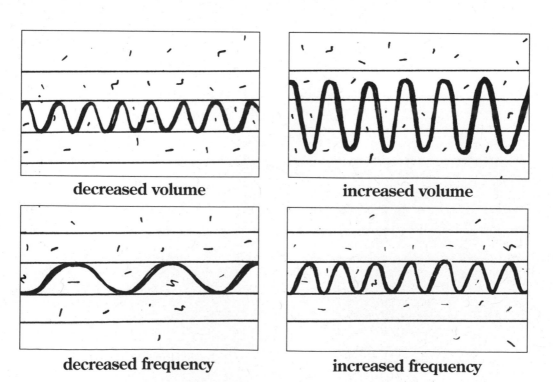

decreased volume

increased volume

decreased frequency

increased frequency

TUNING UP

Have you ever heard your voice on tape? If so, you probably didn't think it sounded like you, but that's the way you sound to other people. When you speak, you hear your own voice vibrating through all the bones of your skull in addition to hearing it with your ears.

Try this test: Hit a kitchen fork on a counter and then clamp your teeth down on the fork. (A tuning fork works even better.) You'll hear the vibrations of sound traveling through your head!

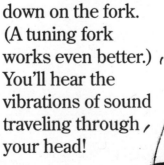

SPINNING AROUND

The three semicircular canals in your inner ear let you know if your body is moving up and down, from side to side or back and forth. Fluid in the canals washes against tiny hairs that send these messages to the brain.

Try spinning around fast enough to move the fluid in your ears. If you stop quickly, the fluid will keep moving and make you dizzy. (Of course, some people enjoy this dizzy sensation—just look at the most popular rides in an amusement park!)

In One Ear and In the Other

Having two ears, instead of one, helps us to locate the sources of sounds. This experiment will show the importance of our binaural (two-eared) system.

You will need:

- A bell or other noisemaker
- A partner
- Tape and markers (optional)

Close your eyes and plug one ear (use your finger or an earplug). Have your partner make a noise, then point in the direction you think it came from. Next, ask your partner to move and make another noise; again, point toward the sound. (To be really scientific, your partner can put tape marks on the floor at the places where the noises are made and drop markers at the places you point out.)

After four or five tries, unplug your ear and try the experiment again. You'll notice quite a difference.

The seashell shape of the human ear is good for picking up sounds. When you hold a seashell up to your own ear, the "ocean" you hear is the sound waves bouncing around inside the shell!

Come to Your Senses

Your senses of hearing, sight, smell, taste and touch tell you about the world around you. Your "sixth sense" (intuition) may come in handy here!

ACROSS

4. Tearful sound
6. Sweet-smelling flower
7. Like the taste of a lemon
9. Crow's sound
10. Sweet-tasting potato
12. Sound of greeting
13. Very attractive
17. "Drink your ____!"
18. Sound of hesitation
19. Dangerously loud
22. Thoughtful sound
24. Very tasty, like chicken
27. Sound of laughter
28. Fingerprinting substance
29. Barking sound
31. Sound carrier
34. Buzzing locale
36. Nuzzled
37. Companion to 21 Down

DOWN

1. Companion to 3 Down
2. Poignant
3. Very appetizing
4. So-____, like some meals
5. Nerve center
8. Attention-getting sounds
10. Cheerleading sound
11. One of Baby's first sounds
14. Puppy's sound
15. Sound of disapproval
16. "Wipe your ____!"
20. ____-tock

21. Very scary
22. Sound of disgust
23. Source of protein
25. Eye wipers
26. "____ a pig's eye!"
30. Number of senses
32. Fire engine color

33. Snake's sound
34. Santa sound
35. Pig's sound
36. Pecan or pistachio, for example

Light Show

Without light, you wouldn't be able to see the color, size or shape of the objects around you. The light that enters the front of your eye through the pupil allows the retina in back to make upside-down "pictures" of the objects, which are then interpreted by your brain.

At the center of the retina are color-sensitive cells called cones; to either side are the rods, which pick out black and white. Do the experiment on the facing page to learn how this configuration affects your vision.

Optic Nerve

Pupil

Lens

Iris

Retina

Cone   Rod

Believe it or not, there are always tears in your eyes! Tears are antiseptic, and their main job is to keep your eyeballs clean. Every time you blink, your eyelids act like windshield wipers, squeezing the extra liquid off to the side. Can you guess how many times you blink in a year?

Answer, page 92

You will need:

- Several different-colored cards or pieces of construction paper
- A chair
- A partner

Sit in the chair, looking forward, and have your partner bring a colored card from behind you out to the side and gradually in front of you. At what point do you first see the card? How long before you can say what color it is?

Because the cones are clustered at the center of the retina, you won't see the color of the card until it comes around to the front.

Now switch places and test your partner's vision with a card of another color.

STAR LIGHT, STAR BRIGHT

Why do even the brightest colors look gray when the lights go out or the sun goes down? Because the color-sensitive cones in the retina of your eye don't work in the dark!

When you look up at a star in the night sky, for example, you'll see it more clearly if you look at it out of the corner of your eye so the rods can pick up its light.

Now You See It, Now You Don't!

Close your left eye, or cover it with your hand, as you hold the book out at arm's length. Focusing on the left-hand image with your right eye, slowly move the book toward your nose. When the image on the right disappears, you've found your "blind spot."

MIRROR CHECK
WHAT BIG EYES YOU HAVE!

Did you ever notice that the pupils of our eyes get bigger and smaller depending on the light? They open wide (dilate) in the dark to let in as much light as possible, allowing us to see, then grow smaller as less light is needed. Stand in front of a mirror in a well-lit room. Keep both eyes open, cover your right eye and count to 20 slowly. Remove your hand and watch your right pupil shrink!

3-D

We're very fortunate to have two eyes. If you had only one eye, like a Cyclops, you'd have a hard time gauging depth and distance. Everything would look two-dimensional, as on a TV screen. To understand the importance of binocular (two-eyed) vision, cover one of your eyes with a patch, or tie a large handkerchief around your head so that it completely covers one eye, and have a friend do the same. Now toss a ball back and forth a few times.

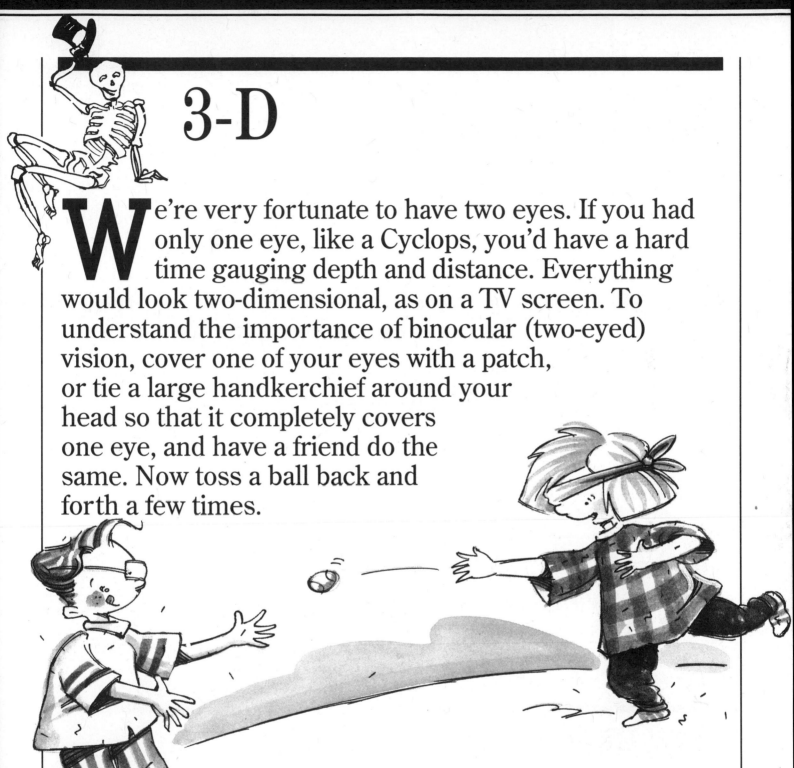

How did you do? (Probably not your best!) Now try again, using both eyes, and see how much easier it is to judge the ball.

Hole-in-One

Here's a way to make it look as if there's a hole in your hand. Roll a piece of paper into a tube and hold it up to one eye. Put your free hand right up against the side of the tube near the end; keeping both eyes open, slide your hand along the tube until it's fairly close to your nose.

At some point, you'll "see" a hole in your hand. One eye is seeing through the tube while the other is seeing a whole hand, and your brain has to put the two images together. Instead of a whole hand, your brain sees a hand with a hole!

SEE HERE!

Our eyes often play tricks called optical illusions. For instance, in the first example below, which line would you say is longer? In the second example, which circle is larger? In the third, where do the circles line up?

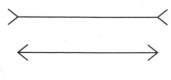

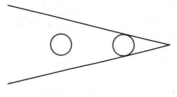

Answers, page 92

The Nose Knows— or Does It?

When you smell an odor, you inhale tiny airborne particles of the odor's source and run them past receptor cells high up in your nose.

Nerves to Brain

Roof of Nose

Receptors

Odors (Chemical Particles)

You can smell as many as 10,000 different odors. But don't ask your nose to do too much at one time, or it will fall asleep on the job!

To see this for yourself, try the test below.

You will need:

- A bottle of vanilla extract or perfume
- A partner

Blindfold your partner and hold the opened bottle of vanilla extract or perfume under his or her nose. Tell your partner to keep sniffing until you take the bottle away. The sniffing will stop before you've moved it, because your partner's "smellers" have gone to sleep.

What's That Smell?

Smell is strongly connected to memory because the centers for each are close together in the brain. So, when you're smelling something you haven't smelled in a while, like grass clippings or your grandmother's kitchen, you can be flooded with memories. To see how this relationship works, try the following experiment.

1. Gather friends or family members around you and show them several objects that don't have smells associated with them. (See below for some ideas.) Then remove the objects from sight, hand out paper and pencils, and ask your test subjects to write down what they saw.

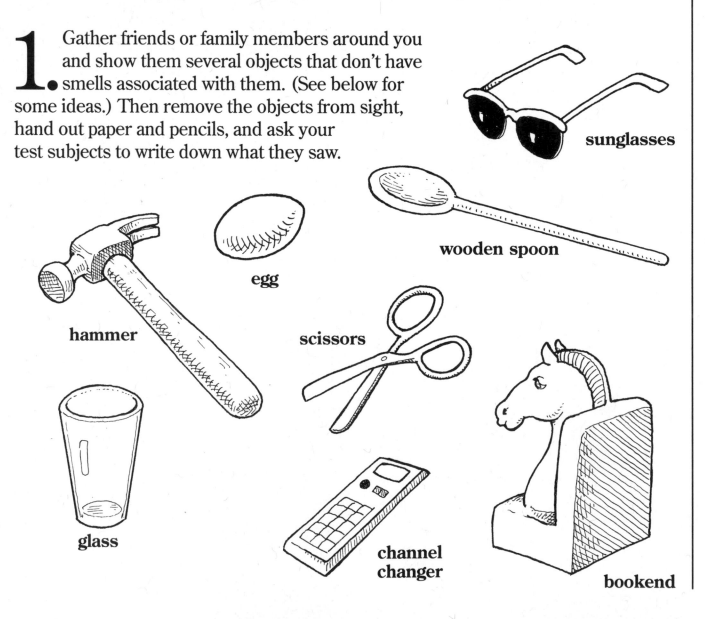

sunglasses

wooden spoon

egg

hammer

scissors

glass

channel changer

bookend

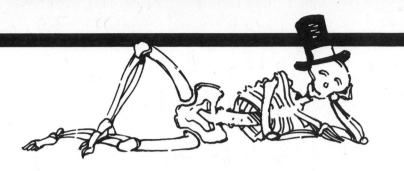

2. Now set out a group of objects such as perfume, garlic, a rose and other items that give off strong odors. Pass them around, then remove them and ask everyone to recall what they were. This time, with memory and smell working together, the answers should be more complete.

Taste Tests

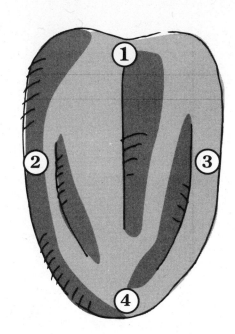

Taste buds are spread out over your tongue like tiny bunches of flowers. There are also a few buds on the roof of your mouth and in such odd places as your pharynx and epiglottis.

Do the tests below to learn some interesting facts about how you taste your food.

Test #1

Your taste buds respond to different tastes—sweet, sour, salt and bitter. To see which part of your tongue is responsible for which tastes, try this experiment.

You will need:

- A cotton swab
- Sugar water (sweet)
- Salt water (salt)
- Vinegar water (sour)
- Unsweetened tea (bitter)

Dab a bit of sugar water on the front, back and two sides of your tongue. Which part of your tongue tastes the sugar's sweetness? Write the word "sweet" next to the appropriate number in the illustration above.

Run the same test with the other solutions. When you're done, you should have a fairly accurate map of your tongue.

Answers, page 92

Test #2

Dry taste buds don't taste anything, as you'll soon see.

You will need:

- Sugar
- A cotton swab

Stick out your tongue and dry it off in the air. Now put some sugar on the tip with the cotton swab. It won't taste sugary until your tongue gets wet.

Test #3

Your sense of taste is greatly influenced by your sense of smell. (When you have a cold, you can lose 80% of your tasting capacity.) To convince yourself, try this experiment.

You will need:

- 2 slices of raw potato

Plug your nose and bite into a slice of raw potato. Does it taste like crunchy nothingness? Now unplug your nose and try the other slice. So that's what raw potato tastes like!

MIRROR CHECK
FUZZY TONGUE!

Check your tongue in the mirror at bedtime. It should be mostly pink, with a whitish stripe down the middle. In the morning, before you brush your teeth, check again. You should see a lot of white "stuff." Try scraping some off with your fingernail. (Don't be squeamish— it's just some harmless mucus and a collection of thousands of skin cells that died during the night!)

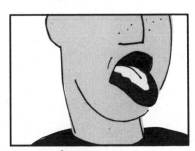

morning

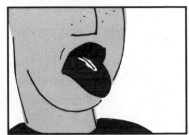

bedtime

55

Jog Your Memory

Doug and Jenny went out for a run and just happened to pass through the street shown below. When they got back home, they couldn't agree on what they saw along the way.

How good is your own memory? Take three minutes to study this scene (much longer than Doug and Jenny had as they blazed down the street). Then turn the page to see how many details you can recall.

Jog Your Memory *(continued)*

Do not read this until you've seen page 56!

- On which building was the clock?
- What time was it?
- What was the name of the fruit store? Was it open or closed?
- What was on sale outside the fruit store?
- What kind of animal was sleeping on the sidewalk?
- How many children were playing on the sidewalk?
- What was the little girl carrying in her basket?
- What was the design on the couple's jackets?
- *Bonus question:* Where was Sherlock Bones?

Answers, page 92

TOTAL RECALL

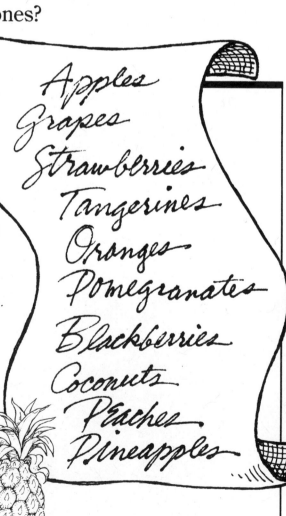

Another way to test your memory is to look at a list of items, then see how many of the items you recognize when they're included in a longer list.

Here is Rosie's list of fruits to order from Farmer Rathbone. Ask a friend to copy the list on a piece of paper, mixing in five *additional* kinds of fruits, while you're out of the room. Then study the list here, close the book and have your friend read the new, *longer* list. Which items were not on Rosie's original list of fruits to order?

Apples
Grapes
Strawberries
Tangerines
Oranges
Pomegranates
Blackberries
Coconuts
Peaches
Pineapples

Chapter 6
All Systems Go

Watering Holes
Just Picture It!
Secret Ingredients
The Whole Tooth
Sound Bites
The Hard Facts
Apple Adventure
Gulp!
Three-Letter Words
Matters of the Heart
Go With the Flow
Wise Guys
Artificial Respiration
All Together Now!

Watering Holes

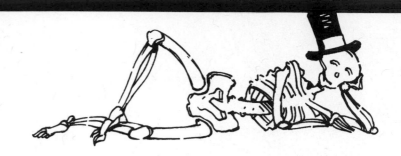

The first step in the digestive process takes place when saliva softens up the food in your mouth and goes to work on the starches, reducing them to simple sugars. (To feel the salivary glands, move your tongue up on the inside of your cheek above your second upper molar.) You can test the effects of saliva by keeping a piece of bread or a soda cracker in your mouth after chewing it thoroughly. Not only will it turn to mush, but you'll detect a sugary flavor!

To see saliva at work, do the following experiment.

You will need:
- Several bowls
- A pan
- Water
- Cornstarch
- Iodine
- Saliva

Check with a parent before you begin.

1. Boil a cup of water and drop in one tablespoon of cornstarch. (Cornstarch is a fairly pure form of starch.) Let the solution cool.

2. Next, collect one tablespoon of saliva and place it in a bowl with two tablespoons of the cooled starch solution.

3. Take out one teaspoon of the mixture; put it in another bowl.

4. Add a drop of iodine. If starch is present, the iodine will turn blue-black.

5. Test the remainder of the solution after 10 minutes. How much starch is left?

Just Picture It!

The strings of pictures and boxes on these pages are called rebus puzzles. To solve them, write the picture-names in the appropriate boxes, then add and subtract letters as shown. You'll end up with the letters of five words—all associated with a single part of the body.

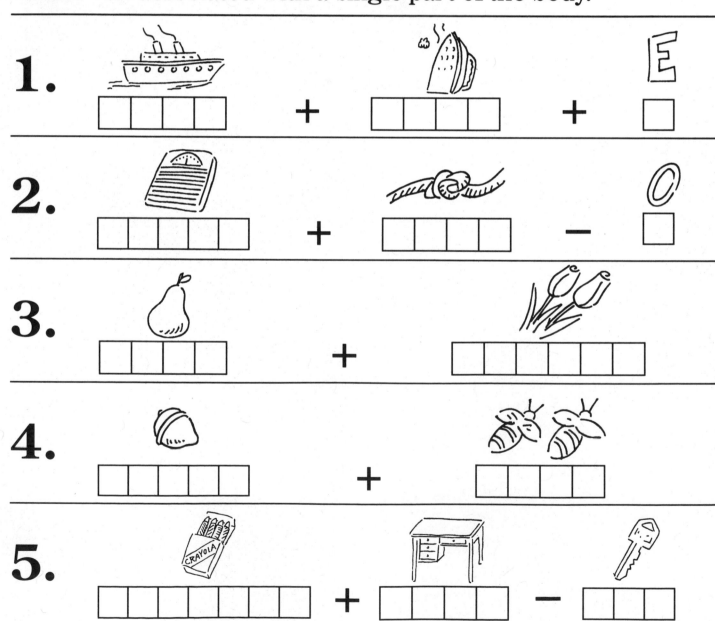

Secret Ingredients

Food provides the energy that keeps all your systems going. You can fill your body's needs best by eating from the four food groups: breads and cereals (4 or more servings per day), fruits and vegetables (5 servings per day), milk products (3 to 4 servings per day), and meats and beans (2 servings per day). These foods contain the carbohydrates, fats and proteins that your body needs to function efficiently.

breads and cereals

fruits and vegetables

milk products

meats and beans

Try these tests on your food to determine its composition.

You will need:

- Squares of brown paper from grocery bags
- Iodine
- Samples of different kinds of food, such as an apple, a doughnut, a potato, peanut butter, cheese and corn chips

To test for fat: Rub the food on a paper square and let the paper dry out. Now hold it up to a light. If you can see the light through the paper, the food contains fat.

To test for carbohydrates (starch): Drop a drop of iodine on the food. If there's starch, the food will turn a blue-black color.

The Whole Tooth

Upper

6–7 years
7–8 years
10–12 years
9–11 years
10–12 years

Lower

10–12 years
9–11 years
9–12 years
7–8 years
6–7 years

O f the 20 teeth in your first set (your "baby teeth"), those at the front are usually the first to go; the last are farther back. These "dropouts" make room for your permanent teeth—all 32 of them!

A good way to take care of your teeth is to cut down on sugary foods. Sugar is food for plaque, which in turn gives off acid that causes cavities. To see how this happens, do the following experiment.

You will need:

- 2 halves of an eggshell
- A jar of water
- A jar of vinegar
- Soda pop

Eggshell makes a good substitute for a tooth because it's made mostly of calcium and so are teeth. (If you've kept a tooth left behind by the tooth fairy, use it in the experiment!) Put one-half of the eggshell in the jar of water and the other half in the vinegar. Leave them overnight. What happens when the acid in the vinegar gets at the shell?

Try the experiment a second time, using soda pop. Does the soda contain enough acid to eat away the eggshell? What does that tell you about drinking a lot of pop?

Sound Bites

Animals have different kinds of teeth, depending on which foods they eat. *Carnivores* eat meat and fish, whereas *herbivores* eat only plants. *Omnivores* eat just about anything. And *insectivores* eat . . . guess what?

Can you match the teeth below with the animals on the left and the foods on the right?

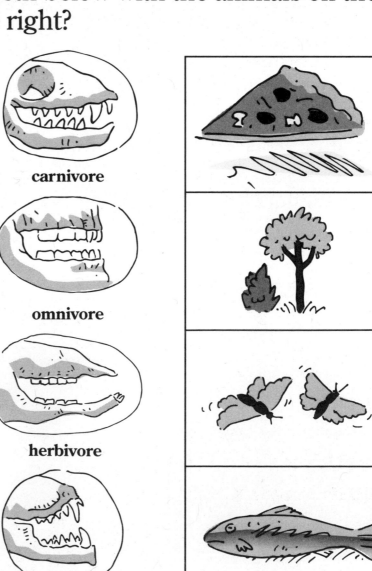

carnivore

omnivore

herbivore

insectivore

The Hard Facts

What is the hardest substance in the human body?

You can find the answer by completing the puzzle below. All the body parts listed at the right can be found in the grid. The words are hidden across, back, up, down and diagonally in the grid. Circle each word that you track down in the grid, then write out the unused letters in order from left to right and top to bottom. These letters will spell out the name of the hardest substance in your body.

ANKLE
ARTERY
BLOOD
EYELASH
FINGERNAIL
HIP
INTESTINE
JAW
KNEECAP
LIGAMENT
LUNG
MUSCLE
NERVE
NOSE
SKULL
TONGUE
VERTEBRA

Answers, page 93

F	T	O	Y	R	E	T	R	A	E
I	I	O	K	T	O	S	J	Y	H
N	A	N	A	N	K	L	E	A	M
T	R	E	G	U	E	L	U	U	W
E	B	U	L	E	A	E	S	N	B
S	E	L	N	S	R	C	C	L	G
T	T	N	H	O	L	N	O	A	A
I	R	M	E	E	S	O	A	L	P
N	E	R	V	E	D	E	H	I	P
E	V	T	N	E	M	A	G	I	L

Apple Adventure

When you eat, you don't have to worry about pointing your food in the right direction. Your body takes care of it, pushing it through all the right tubes at the right time. In this maze, however, it's not that easy— we've drawn in a few dead ends! Can you lead the apple safely through the digestive tract without getting stuck in places like the appendix or the gall bladder?

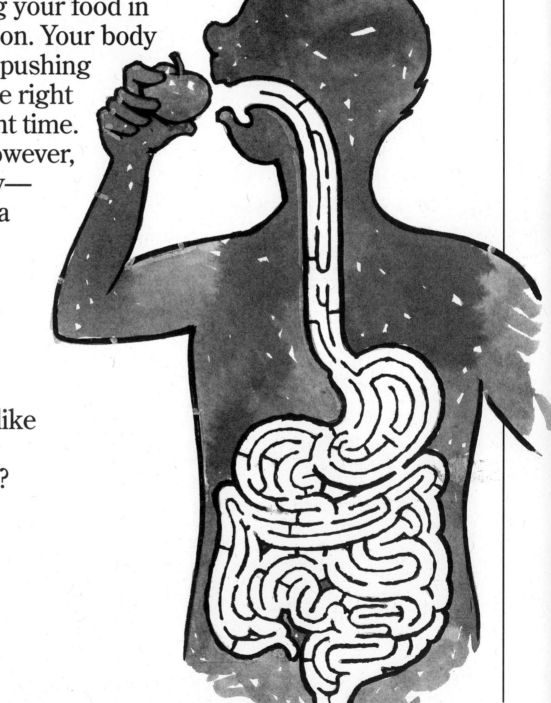

Answers, page 93

Gulp!

Here's a word puzzle that should be easy to digest. A bite of hamburger, already chewed and softened in the oral cavity (the mouth), can't begin its trip through the body until you fill in the remaining parts of the digestive system, one letter per box. Boxes that contain the same letter are connected by lines. Using the first set of lines as your starting point, see if you can fill in all the blanks to trace the burger's path from start to finish.

Answers, page 93

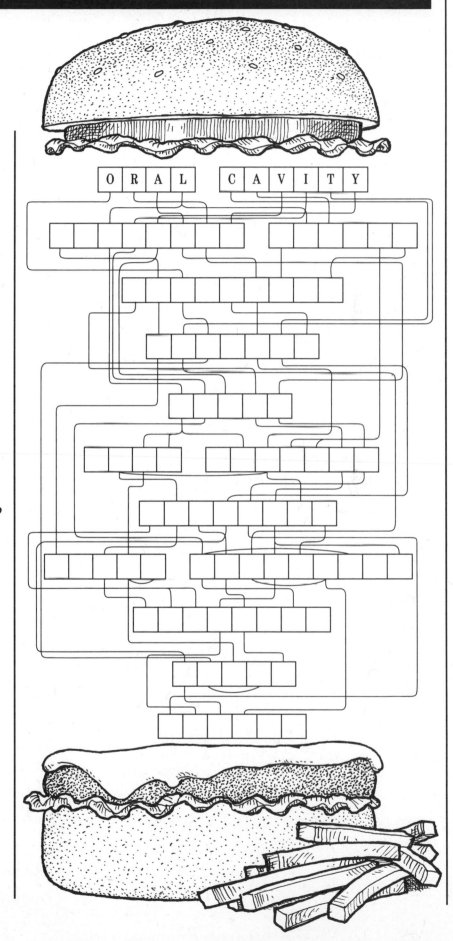

O R A L   C A V I T Y

Three-Letter Words

Ten of the three-letter words hidden below are ordinary names for parts of the body. To find these words, go from one letter to any letter next to it (even diagonally) and then on to a letter next to that one. You may go back to a letter (BIB would be a good answer, if it were a part of the body), but you may not use a letter twice in a row (EGG is not an allowed answer).

Happy hunting!

T	Y	L	B
O	E	I	P
G	R	A	H
U	M	J	W

Matters of the Heart

Your doctor uses a stethoscope to listen to your heart, where two pumps control the flow of blood through the body. To make a model stethoscope so you can hear these pumps at work, follow the directions below and ask a friend to be your "patient."

You will need:

- A large plastic soda bottle (or a funnel)
- A piece of rubber tubing from a hardware store (or the cardboard cylinder inside a roll of paper towels or wrapping paper)

Cut off the top of the bottle just where it reaches its widest point. Squeeze the hose into the opening. (Make certain it fits snugly.)

Now find a quiet room and place the wide end of your stethoscope on the upper-left side of your friend's chest; put the other end to your ear. You should hear two separate noises, often referred to as "lub-dub" because of the way they sound. The "lub" part of the heartbeat is the sound of valves shutting as blood from the lungs or veins enters the heart. The "dub" is the sound of valves shutting at the top of the heart as blood leaves one of the ventricles to go to the lungs or arteries.

Go With the Flow

A system of muscles and valves gives the blood in your veins the extra push it needs to get back up to your heart, particularly from faraway places like your feet. The valves allow the blood to travel in only one direction and keep it from flowing backwards.

Can you get Ernie Erythrocyte from the foot at the bottom of the page up to the heart at the top?

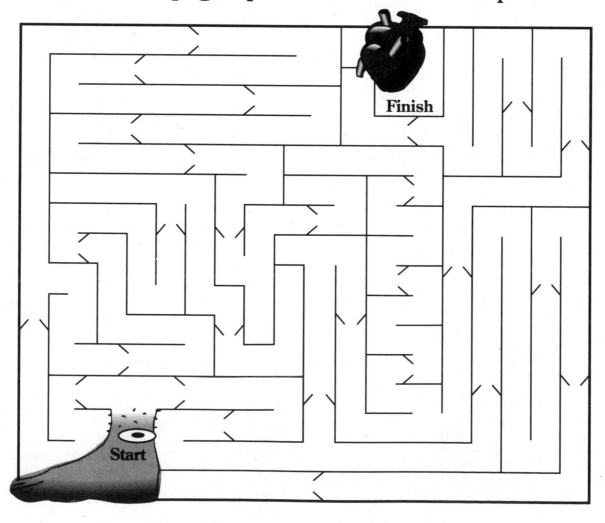

Wise Guys

To discover the fact hidden in the puzzle below, first fill in as many definitions as you can. Next, transfer each letter to the corresponding square in the grid. (See the first letter of Definition F and its place in the grid.) The completed grid will spell out a question. Reading down, the first letters of the filled-in definitions will spell out the answer!

Definitions

a. Victory hand-slap (2 wds.) ....
17 24 40 58 14 29 30 53

b. Long-armed great ape ....
15 16 64 42 26 43 35 3 46

c. Mouth-to-_____ resuscitation ....
19 70 18 7 61

d. Sidelined, as in football (3 wds.) ....
56 25 55 38 23 33 50 9 51 2

e. Nickname for a family member ....
32 59 44

f. Hard-working insects ....
A 45 10 37 27

g. Small stone ....
49 31 67 22 65 41

h. Reykjavik's island republic ....
52 60 13 66 6 71 47

i. Cake ingredients (2 wds.) ....
63 72 28 57 36 8 4 39 54

j. Jane or James, for example ....
21 11 12 68

k. Gulp ....
48 62 20 69 5 34 1

1 K	2 D	3 B	4 I		5 K	6 H	7 C	8 I	9 D		10 F	11 J	12 J	13 H
	14 A	15 B	16 B		17 A	18 C	19 C	20 K	21 J		22 G	23 D	24 A	25 D
26 B	27 F		28 I	29 A	30 A	31 G	32 E		33 D	34 K	35 B	36 I		37 F
38 D	39 I		40 A	41 G	42 B	43 B	44 E		45 F A	46 B	47 H		48 K	49 G
50 D	51 D	52 H	53 A	54 I		55 D	56 D		57 I	58 A	59 E	60 H	61 C	
62 K	63 I		64 B	65 G	66 H		67 G	68 J	69 K	70 C	71 H	72 I	?	

Answers, page 94

Artificial Respiration

By the time you reach adulthood, your lungs will weigh about two pounds. The only organs that float, lungs take in the oxygen that you need for energy and rid your body of a waste gas called carbon dioxide. Air entering your trachea travels through the lobes until it reaches the alveoli, which transfer oxygen to the bloodstream and pick up unwanted CO_2 for disposal.

To better understand how you breathe, make a model of one lung as shown here.

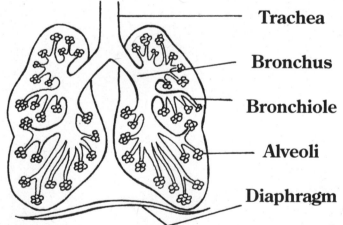

- Trachea
- Bronchus
- Bronchiole
- Alveoli
- Diaphragm

You will need:

- A see-through plastic bottle with lid
- A straw
- 2 balloons (1 large, 1 small)
- 2 rubber bands
- Clay

1. Cut the bottom off the bottle and punch a hole in the lid. Cut open the large balloon and spread it out to cover the opening at the bottom of the bottle; seal it tight with a rubber band. Holding the lid separately, put the straw through the hole and attach the small balloon to one end with clay. (Use a twisted rubber band if it doesn't fit snugly.) Put the top on the bottle and seal it tight with clay.

2. To watch the lung work, push on the diaphragm (the balloon at the bottom of the bottle). You should see the balloon shrivel when the diaphragm rises and fill out again when the diaphragm is relaxed.

3. Now blow into the tip of the straw. You should see the diaphragm expand and the lung inflate.

Feel your own chest as you breathe deeply; does it work the same way?

MIRROR CHECK
ALL STEAMED UP

Each time you exhale, tiny drops of water in your breath carry heat from your body to help control its temperature. Put your face close to a mirror and breathe hard through your mouth. The "fog" that you'll see on the mirror is evaporated water, or water vapor. Every day, you breathe out about a pint of water this way!

75

All Together Now!

Systems are the largest labor divisions in your body. The smallest workers are the cells, which work alone or join together to form tissues; next largest are the organs, which can be grouped together in systems. For example, the heart, veins and arteries all help to circulate blood, so they belong to the circulatory system.

How many of the systems named below can you locate in the grid? Look for words reading across, back, up, down and diagonally.

CIRCULATORY

DIGESTIVE

ENDOCRINE

MUSCULAR

NERVOUS

REPRODUCTIVE

RESPIRATORY

SKELETAL

URINARY

K	E	L	E	N	I	R	C	O	D	N	E
S	R	E	P	R	O	D	U	C	T	V	N
T	S	E	V	I	T	S	E	G	I	D	U
N	D	E	S	S	K	I	N	T	I	K	R
I	E	L	G	P	N	D	C	G	M	S	I
R	M	R	A	I	I	U	I	U	S	U	N
U	N	E	V	T	D	R	S	G	T	O	A
S	U	O	V	O	E	C	A	S	E	V	R
C	C	I	R	C	U	L	A	T	O	R	Y
U	D	P	G	L	C	S	E	D	O	E	O
L	E	N	A	I	U	N	I	K	O	R	R
R	O	R	E	N	D	O	C	R	S	T	Y

Answers, page 94

Chapter 7

Body Works

Blue Genes
Bodily Myths
Little Man
Is There a Doctor in the House?
Dizzying Heights
Balance of Power

Blue Genes

The way you look depends partly on the combinations of genes inside each cell of your body. According to these "blueprints," handed down from your parents, you might have red hair and freckles, or brown eyes and long lashes, or big ears and a cute button nose.

Mrs. Bones, the science teacher at Lower Molar School, used her knowledge of genes on Parents' Night when all the name tags disappeared. To match the mothers and fathers with the right students, she made a mental list of the dominant genes that parents pass on to their children. From the list below and the parents pictured at the right, can you make the correct deductions?

- Brown hair is dominant over blond hair
- Dimples are dominant over no dimples
- Freckles are dominant over no freckles
- Extra-long eyelashes are dominant over shorter lengths
- Brown eyes are dominant over blue eyes

Jessica

Rob

Gilbert

Answers, page 95

GENETIC CODE

Are there any twins in your family? If so, the tendency to have twins is inherited, and someday you just might produce your own perfect pair of look-alikes!

An anecdote about twins is written in code below. One word has already been decoded, so you can start by writing the letter "T" under each letter "J," and so on.

Use your detective skills to break the code and fill in the rest of the story.

K LAUKW QZJ MZB

PBAJMZB WKUZ MZB

JLSWG. AWZ LKG K
TWINS

VSBQ KWO AWZ LKG K

PAC. JMZ TWXQZ

XKQQZO JMZU OZWSGZ

KWO OZWZRMZL!

Answers, page 95

The Olds

The Hodes

The Mannings

Bodily Myths

Have you ever wondered if all the DOs and DON'Ts you've grown up with are based on fact? Well, as you'll soon find out, some are—and some aren't!

True   False

1. Eating watermelon seeds can cause watermelon plants to grow inside you.

2. You shouldn't swim until at least an hour after you've eaten.

3. You should "feed a cold" (eat and drink more) and "starve a fever" (eat and drink less).

4. If you get haircuts frequently, your hair will grow faster.

5. There are more cold viruses in winter than in any other season.

6. You can't get sunburned on a cloudy day.

7. It's soothing to drink milk before bed.

8. When you wrinkle from spending a long time in a bathtub or pool, it's because your skin has soaked up a lot of water.

9. Eating too much sugar can cause acne.

10. If you cross your eyes one too many times, they'll get stuck that way.

Answers, page 95

Little Man

Before modern science, people believed that a tiny human being was outlined in each person's cells so the body would know how to develop. They named this being from the Latin word for "little man." Solve the puzzle below to discover the word for yourself. It appears at 23 Across.

ACROSS
1. Smallest particle
5. Arm joint
10. Couch
11. Sister's daughter
12. Trick
13. Flaws in a fender
14. "___ a dog's life."
16. Goo
19. Parts of a minute (abbr.)
23. ? ? ?
25. Test
26. Foot joint
27. Jack ___ Jill
28. Following
32. Wicked
36. Heavy milk
37. Bat's home
38. Layers, as on a cake
39. Leg joint

DOWN
1. Cinder
2. Also
3. One ___ kind (2 wds.)
4. Largest capacity
5. Odds and ___
6. Fib
7. Big ___ (clock in London, England)
8. Month after September (abbr.)
9. Nickname for Wesley
15. Number of fingers on both hands
16. Female pronoun
17. ___ and bagels
18. "___ Yankee Doodle Dandy" (2 wds.)
19. Place to get a tan
20. Large member of the deer family
21. ___-de-sac
22. Compass direction (from New York City to Washington, D.C., for example)
24. Tin container
27. Upper limbs
28. One of the sections of a play
29. Day before Saturday (abbr.)
30. Tiny stand for a golf ball
31. Location of semicircular canals
33. Large vehicle
34. "___ been working on the railroad"
35. Robert E. ___

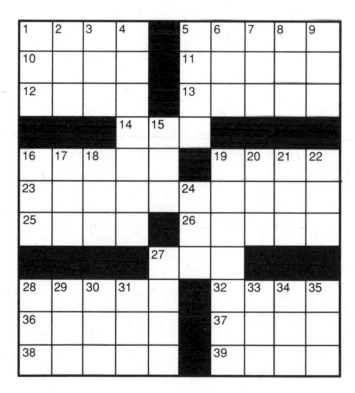

Is There a Doctor in the House?

The directory in the lobby of the Pettibone Medical Center lists the following doctors and the branches of medicine they practice:

- Dr. Black, Cardiology
- Dr. Brown, Podiatry
- Dr. Gold, Dermatology

- Dr. Green, Ophthalmology
- Dr. Silver, Obstetrics
- Dr. White, Orthopedics

Examine the doctors' offices shown on these pages. Can you place each doctor in the proper office?

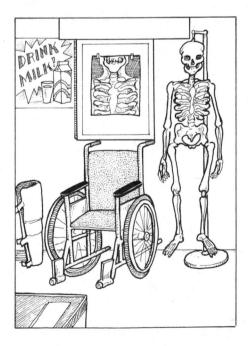

Dr. _____

Dr. _____

Answers, page 96

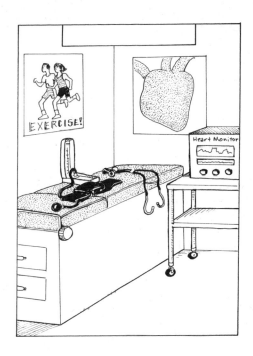

Dr. _____

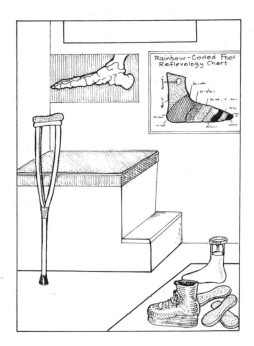

Dr. _____

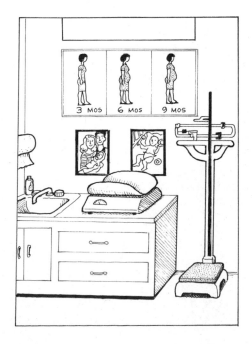

Dr. _____

Dr. _____

Dizzying Heights

In your first year of life, you tripled your weight and grew half again as tall as you were at birth. Sometime between age 10 and age 15, another growth spurt could add another four to six inches to your height in a single year. Your head, hands and feet will reach their full size first, so don't be alarmed if they look too big for your body—you're just growing into them!

How tall are you now? Here's a scientific method that uses bone measurements to calculate height.

You will need:

- A tape measure or ruler
- A pencil and paper
- An adult partner

Ask your partner to measure your arm from the shoulder joint to the bump on the near side of your elbow, then write down the number of inches in the appropriate space on the facing page. This figure represents the length of your humerus, or upper arm bone.

FOR GIRLS

Length of humerus: _____inches (cm)

Multiply this figure by 3.14

Add 25.58 (or 65 cm)

FOR BOYS

Length of humerus: _____inches (cm)

Multiply this figure by 2.97

Add 28.96 (or 73.5 cm)

The final figure will give you your height in inches (or centimeters). Now take the measurements of your partner's upper arm and see what answers you get using the calculations above.

MORNING STRETCH

At bedtime, ask a family member to hold a book flat on the top of your head and mark your height with a light pencil line on the wall. The next morning, when you first get up, measure again. You'll be taller! Overnight, the disks that separate the vertebrae in your spine swelled up with water that will be squeezed out during the day by gravity and physical exercise.

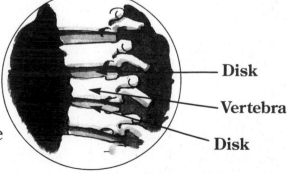

Disk

Vertebra

Disk

Can you guess how many vertebrae you have in all?

Answer, page 96

Balance of Power

Even at a standstill, your body has to send millions of messages through your nervous system just to keep you in the same position. So you can imagine the huge flurry of messages required to move your body from one place to another! To see what happens when some of these important communications are missing, try the following experiment.

You will need:

- A blindfold
- A ball of string or a bunch of rags
- A large, open space (a field or parking lot)
- A partner

Set a goal to walk to—say, a big tree—across the open space. Put on the blindfold and start walking toward your goal. Have your partner follow along to make sure you don't trip on anything or fall down a rabbit hole. Your partner should also unwind the string as you go or drop rags every few feet to mark the path you take.

When you think you're close to your goal, stop. Remove the blindfold and look back at your path. Without messages from the eyes to the brain, the sense of direction goes awry, and most blindfolded people will walk in a circle when they think they're walking straight!

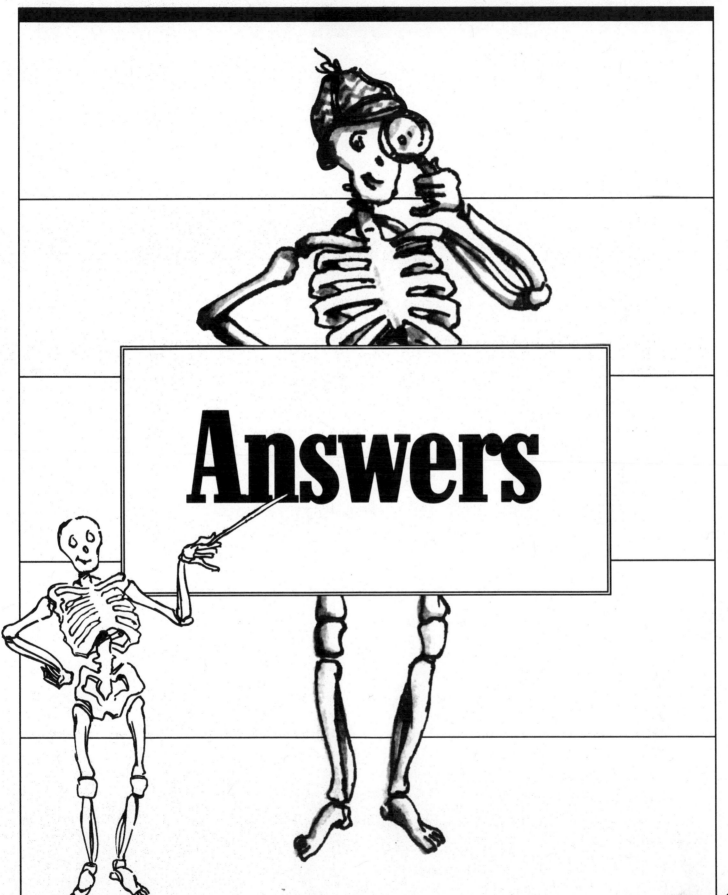

Answers

Chapter 1: The Bone Zone

Bones to Pick *(page 10)*

Only skeletons ⓓ and ⓔ will pass inspection. Skeleton ⓐ is missing the thumb of the right hand; Skeleton ⓑ is missing the knee joint of the left leg; and Skeleton ⓒ is missing a section of the spine.

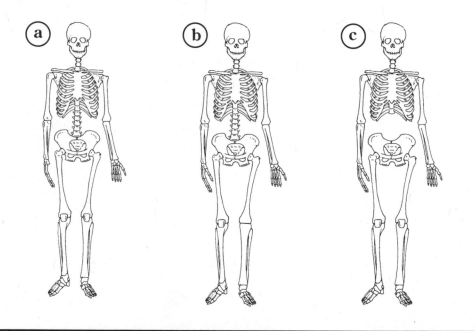

Meet Me at the Joint *(page 11)*

The Knuckle Joint ① is at Metacarpals and Phalanges
The Wrist Joint ② is at Carpals and Radius/Ulna
The Ankle Joint ③ is at Tarsals and Tibia/Fibula
The Knee Joint ④ is at Femur and Tibia/Fibula
The Shoulder Joint ⑤ is at Scapula and Humerus
The Elbow Joint ⑥ is at Humerus and Radius/Ulna
The Hip Joint ⑦ is at Ischium and Femur

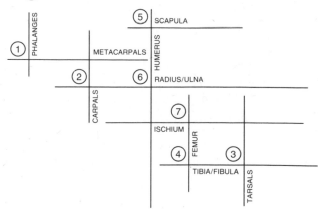

A Pile of Bones *(page 15)*

skull and crossbones

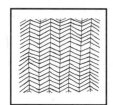

herringbone

lazybones

T-bone

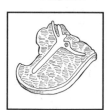

trombone

wishbone

Inside Out *(page 16)*

"I am a <u>grasshopper</u>." The grasshopper is an insect that grows an exoskeleton on the outside of its body.

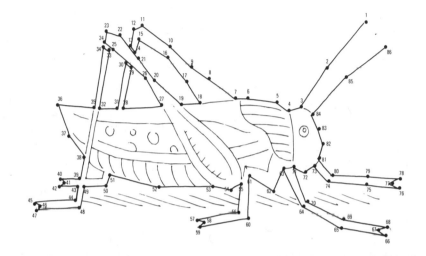

Muscle Mambo *(page 18)*

The smallest muscles in the human body are found in the ear, where the smallest bones (the malleus, incus and stapes) are located.

Handy Dandy

(page 21)

We found the following objects and activities whose names contain the word HAND:

<u>hand</u>bag

<u>hand</u>cuffs   <u>hand</u> puppet

<u>hand</u>kerchief   <u>hand</u>rail

<u>hand</u>les   <u>hand</u>s
*(on garbage   (on people and
can and on   on wristwatch)*
briefcase)*
                    <u>hand</u>shake

<u>hand</u>lebars   <u>hand</u>stand

Organ-ization
(page 24)

a. STOMACH   **b.** BRAIN

c. LUNGS   **d.** HEART

Organ Grinders
(page 25)

1 = b (Your stomach can stretch to hold one quart, or one liter, of food.)

2 = c (Each of your lungs is the size of a football.)

3 = a (Your largest internal organ is the liver.)

4 = b (At rest, your heart beats approximately 75 times per minute.)

5 = b (The size of a person's brain does not determine the degree of his or her intelligence.)

Playing with Instruments
(page 26)

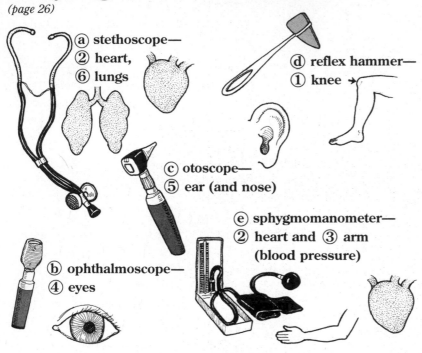

(a) stethoscope—
② heart,
⑥ lungs

(d) reflex hammer—
① knee →

(c) otoscope—
⑤ ear (and nose)

(e) sphygmomanometer—
② heart and ③ arm
(blood pressure)

(b) ophthalmoscope—
④ eyes

Physical Examination
(page 30)

1 = foot
2 = eyes
3 = heel
4 = lip
5 = hand
6 = nails
7 = neck
8 = head
9 = trunk
10 = arm
11 = leg
12 = shoulder

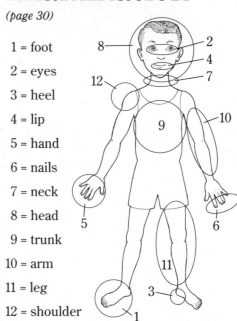

Name Calling (page 28)

1 = a (**The hippocampus** is located in the brain and plays a role in learning and memory.)

2 = c (**Osteoblast** means "bone maker" and describes the cell that helps repair damaged bone and create new bone tissue.)

3 = b (**Pinna** means "feather" or "wing" and refers to the ear lobe.)

4 = a (**The cauda equina** is a spindly bunch of nerve cells that hang down from the spinal cord.)

5 = b (**Solar plexus** means "star-shaped nerve fibers" and is located behind the stomach.)

6 = a (**The Islets of Langerhorn** are the places in the pancreas where insulin is secreted.)

7 = b (**Malleus** means "hammer," the shape of a tiny bone in the ear.)

8 = c (**Duodenum** means "twelve each" ("twelve-finger width") and is the first part of the small intestine, which is about 10 inches, or 25 centimeters, long.)

Body Language (page 32)

1 = i (scapula = shoulder blade)

2 = f (patella = kneecap)

3 = a (pollex = thumb)

4 = j (thorax = chest)

5 = b (larynx = voice box)

6 = e (clavicle = collarbone)

7 = o (tympanum = eardrum)

8 = n (nares = nostrils)

9 = g (tibia = shinbone)

10 = h (coccyx = tailbone)

11 = m (epidermis = skin)

12 = d (sternum = breastbone)

13 = c (trachea = windpipe)

14 = k (phalanx = finger bone)

15 = l (mandible = jawbone)

Have Patients *(page 33)*

We found 16 things wrong with this picture. How many did you find?

1. The numbers on the clock are in the wrong places.
2. The receptionist is speaking into a banana instead of a telephone.
3. The bottom half of the receptionist's body is on the wrong side of the wall.
4. The chair is equipped with a safety belt.
5. There's a bathtub in the doctor's waiting room.
6. The stool has three instead of four legs.
7. The plant is upside down.
8. There's a cat in the aquarium.
9. The man's arm in the sling has three hands.
10. There's a shoe on the man's left arm.
11. There's a hand where a foot should be on the man's left leg.
12. The hat on the man's head is upside down.
13. The eye chart is backwards.
14. There's an exit sign on the front door.
15. There are band-aids instead of hinges on the door.
16. There's a car parked in the hall outside the doctor's office.

How Much, How Many? *(page 34)*

1 = a (1.2 to 1.6 gallons [*5 to 6 l*] = amount of blood in the body)

2 = f (1,000 = number of nerve endings in one square inch of skin)

3 = h (2,000 to 3,000 gallons [*757 to 1,136 kl*] = amount of air an adult breathes per day)

4 = i (60% = percentage of body weight that is water)

5 = e (2.5 pints [*1 l*] = average amount of water sweated per day)

6 = l (44 gallons [*165 l*] = amount of water that passes through the kidneys per day)

7 = k (16% = percentage of body weight that is bone)

8 = c (15 to 30 feet [*5 to 9 m*] = length of the small intestine)

9 = b (1 to 1.5 pints [*.5 to .75 l*] = capacity of the bladder)

10 = j (14% = percentage of body weight that is skin)

11 = g (1 to 2 quarts [*1 to 2 l*] = amount salivated per day)

12 = d (2 to 3 million = number of new red blood cells made per second)

Chapter 4: Cover-Ups

Hairy Tails *(page 39)*

Rapunzel is 200 years old. The prince could weigh 17,500 pounds (or 7,937 kg) and still be supported by her hair.

Pressure Points
(page 40)

The lips have the most touch receptors. **91**

Chapter 5: The Sense of It All

Come to Your Senses *(page 45)*

Light Show *(page 46)*

You blink approximately 10 million times in one year.

See Here! *(page 50)*

The two lines are the same length.

The two circles are the same size.

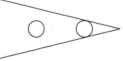

The tops of the circles form a straight line.

○○○○○○○○○

Taste Tests *(page 54)*

The taste map of your tongue should read as follows:

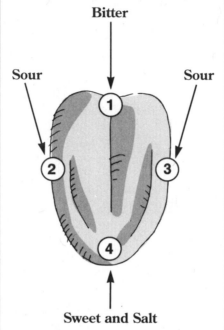

Bitter

Sour   Sour

Sweet and Salt

Jog Your Memory *(page 56)*

- The clock was on the City Hall building.
- The time was 5:05.
- The fruit store was named Rosie's Fruit Store. The store was open.
- Peaches were on sale.
- A dog was sleeping on the sidewalk.
- Three children were playing on the sidewalk.
- The little girl was carrying a kitten in her basket.
- The design on the couple's jackets was a star.
- Sherlock Bones was behind the tree in Alton Park.

Chapter 6: All Systems Go

Just Picture It! *(page 62)*

1. IRON + SHIP + E - PHONE = IRIS

2. SCALE + KNOT - O - TACK = LENS

3. PEAR + TULIPS - TEARS = PUPIL

4. ACORN + BEES - BEAR = CONES

5. CRAYONS + DESK - KEY - CANS = RODS

Sound Bites *(page 66)*

carnivore

sea lion

fish

herbivore

deer

shrubs

omnivore

human

pizza

insectivore

bat

moths

Apple Adventure *(page 68)*

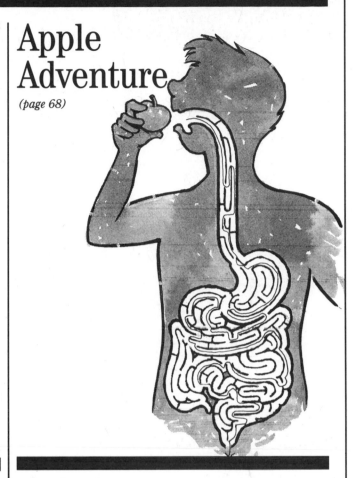

The Hard Facts *(page 67)*

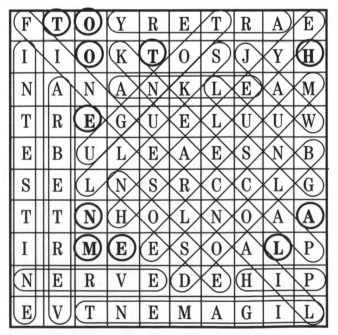

TOOTH ENAMEL

Gulp! *(page 69)*

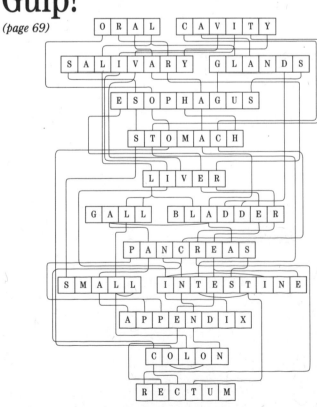

ORAL CAVITY
SALIVARY GLANDS
ESOPHAGUS
STOMACH
LIVER
GALL BLADDER
PANCREAS
SMALL INTESTINE
APPENDIX
COLON
RECTUM

93

Three-Letter Words
(page 70)

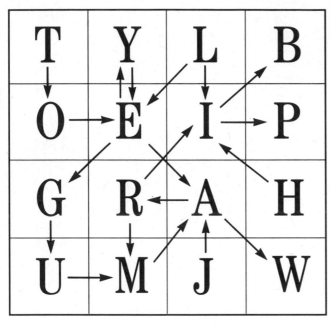

ARM, EAR, EYE, GUM, HIP, JAW, LEG,
LIP, RIB, TOE

Wise Guys *(page 73)*

The answer to the question spelled out in the
grid is **HOMO SAPIENS** (see the first letters
of the answers to the clues below).

a. HIGH FIVE   e. SIS
b. ORANGUTAN   f. ANTS
c. MOUTH   g. PEBBLE
d. ON THE BENCH   h. ICELAND
                     i. EGG WHITES
                     j. NAME
                     k. SWALLOW

1K W	2D H	3B A	4I T		5K L	6H A	7C T	8I I	9D N		10F N	11J A	12J M	13H E
	14A F	15B O	16B R		17A H	18C U	19C M	20K A	21J N		22G B	23D E	24A I	25D N
26B G	27F S			28I G	29A I	30A V	31G E	32E S		33D B	34K O	35B T	36I H		37F T
38D H	39I E		40A G	41G E	42B N·	43B U	44E S		45F A	46B N	47H D		48K S	49G P
50D E	51D C	52H I	53A E	54I S		55D T	56D O		57I W	58A H	59E I	60H C	61C H
62K W	63I E		64B A	65G L	66H L		67G B	68J E	69K L	70C O	71H N	72I G	?

Go With the Flow *(page 72)*

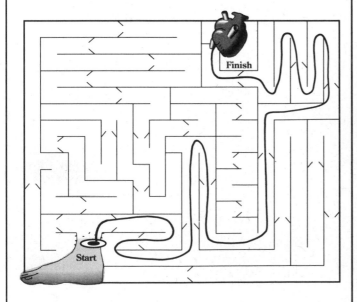

All Together Now! *(page 76)*

K	E	L	E	N	I	R	C	O	D	N	E
S	R	E	P	R	O	D	U	C	T	V	N
T	S	E	V	I	T	S	E	G	I	D	U
N	D	E	S	S	K	I	N	T	I	K	R
I	E	L	G	P	N	D	C	G	M	S	I
R	M	R	A	I	I	U	I	U	S	U	N
U	N	E	V	T	D	R	S	G	T	O	A
S	U	O	V	O	F	C	A	S	E	V	R
C	C	I	R	C	U	L	A	T	O	R	Y
U	D	P	G	L	C	S	E	D	O	E	O
L	E	N	A	I	U	N	I	K	O	R	R
R	O	R	E	N	D	O	C	R	S	T	Y

Chapter 7: Body Works

Blue Genes *(page 78)*

Jessica has dimples, light hair and long eyelashes. Her parents must be the Mannings.

Rob has freckles and dark hair. His parents must be the Hodes.

Gilbert has dimples and light hair. His parents must be the Olds.

The Mannings   **The Olds**

The Hodes

Genetic Code *(page 79)*

The decoded anecdote reads as follows:

A woman let her brother name her twins. One was a girl and one was a boy. The uncle called them Denise and Denephew!

CODE:

K = A	M = H
L = W	B = R
A = O	P = B
U = M	S = I
W = N	G = S
Q = L	C = Y
Z = E	O = D
J = T	V = G
	T = U

Bodily Myths *(page 80)*

1. **False.** Watermelon seeds (or any other seeds) will not grow inside you.
2. **True.** The stomach can cramp if blood helping you to digest is pulled to muscles needed for swimming.
3. **False.** You should feed both a cold and a fever. Your body needs energy to fight infection.
4. **False.** Your hair grows at the same rate whether or not you cut it.
5. **False.** Although in winter you spend more time indoors, breathing in viruses, you're no more at risk than in any other season.
6. **False.** Ultra-violet rays come through clouds, so you can get sunburned on a cloudy day.
7. **True.** Milk helps the release of a tranquilizing substance in your body.
8. **True.** Your skin cells become swollen and bunch together, and this is what causes wrinkles.
9. **False.** Acne is not caused by eating too much sugar.
10. **False.** Crossing your eyes will not make them stick that way.

Little Man *(page 81)*

A	T	O	M		E	L	B	O	W
S	O	F	A		N	I	E	C	E
H	O	A	X		D	E	N	T	S
			I	T	S				
S	L	I	M	E		S	E	C	S
H	O	M	U	N	C	U	L	U	S
E	X	A	M		A	N	K	L	E
			A	N	D				
A	F	T	E	R		E	V	I	L
C	R	E	A	M		C	A	V	E
T	I	E	R	S		K	N	E	E

Is There a Doctor in the House? *(page 82)*

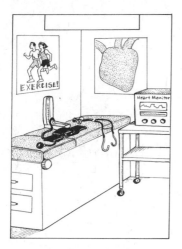

Dr. Black, Cardiology

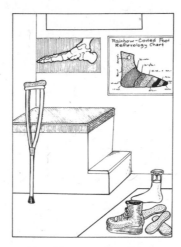

Dr. Brown, Podiatry

Dr. Gold, Dermatology

Dr. Green, Ophthalmology

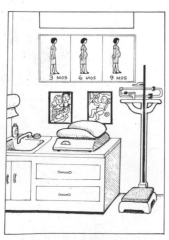

Dr. Silver, Obstetrics

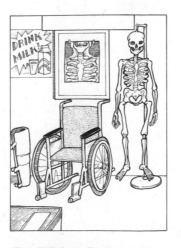

Dr. White, Orthopedics

Morning Stretch

(page 85)

You have 33 vertebrae (24 separate vertebrae plus the fused vertebrae of your sacrum and coccyx).

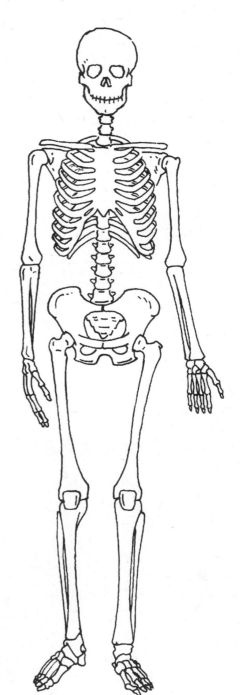